30 Days of Coloring Books for Kids and Adults

Book 5

By Gary Wittmann

First Published, 2018

Printed in the United States of America

Please use light color pencil or crayons or fine markers, there is a blank page following the drawing. You may wish to put something under the page to prevent bleeding.

Thanks for buying this ebook.

Join us on Facebook:

https://www.facebook.com/30DaysofColoringBooksForKidsandAdults/

We will start to have some Facebook Live Coloring Pages.

This link will help your sign up to our newsletter.

http://bit.ly/2C92vYS

copy and paste into your browser.

This is a group of Patterns, Titles and More.

Reasons to play with Coloring books.

1. **Coloring helps you unwind.**

   Let's face it—at the end of the day our lives are filled with deadlines. Sitting down and just unwind with our creative process helps us.

2. **Coloring stimulates your right brain and helps you think more clearly.**

   Research shows you are more creative when your right brain is stimulated.

3. **Coloring makes for a fun night in with friends.**

   Great time is with your family or friends doing what you may in loving to draw and talk and have fun.

4. **Coloring is a great creative outlet.**

   It doesn't matter about your artistic ability. It doesn't matter about your letting the sky be blue or green. You get to do what you feel.

5. **Coloring books makes the perfect gift.**

   Recently at a get together, I had a present for everyone who came to our party. It was a box of coloring books and crayons and markers. Everyone laugh so hard and talk more than if we were playing cards.

Book 5 Patterns and Tiles

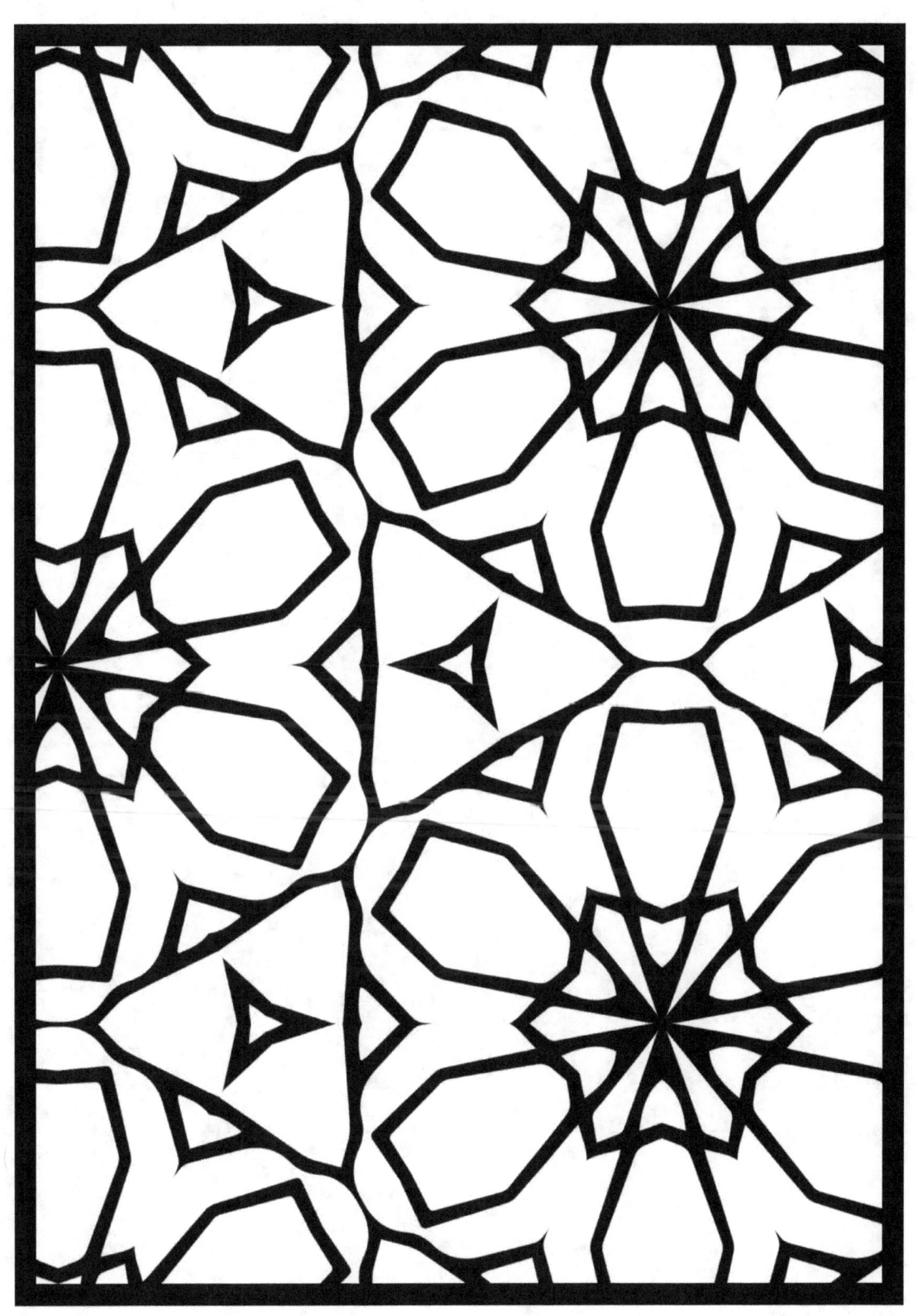

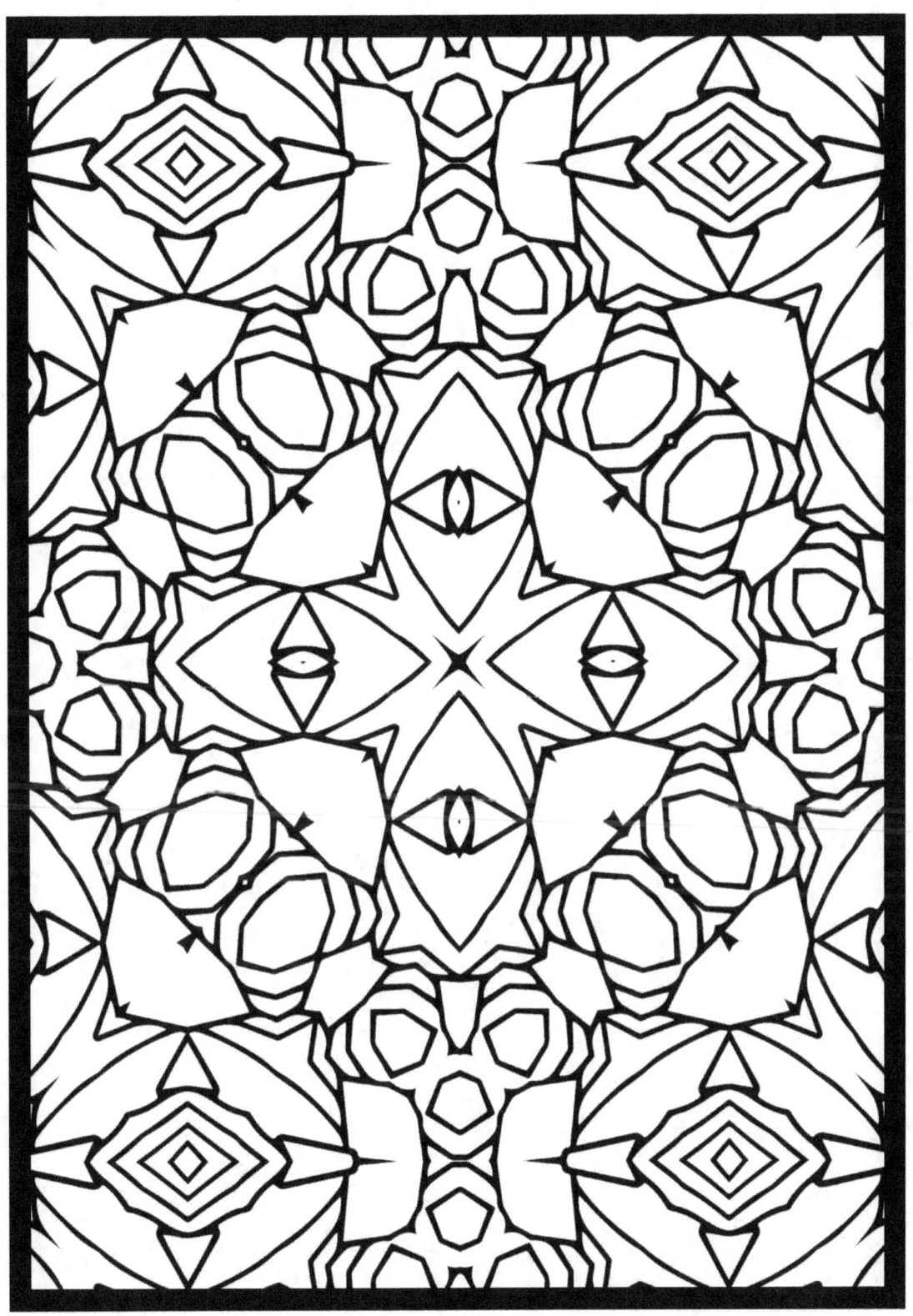

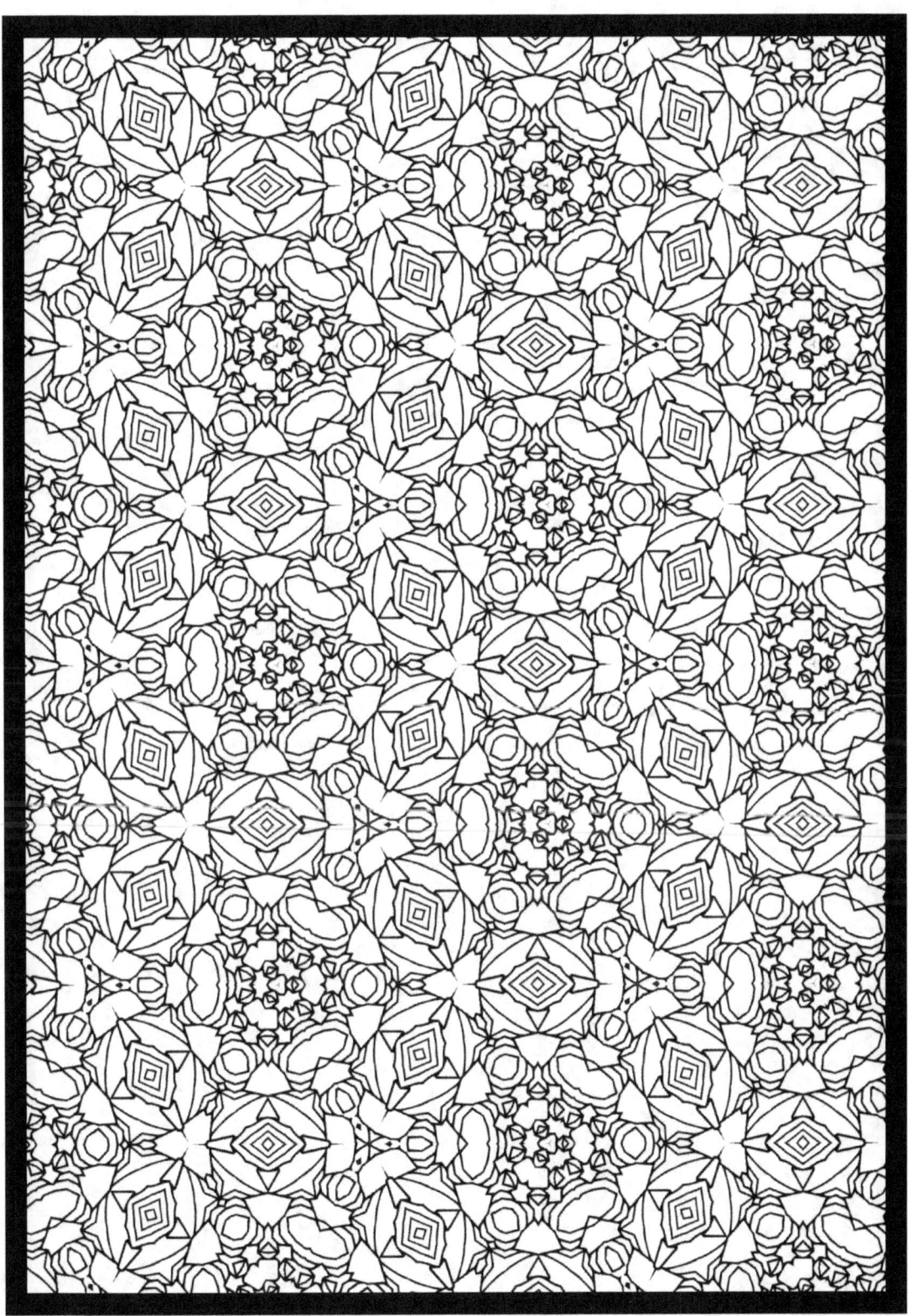

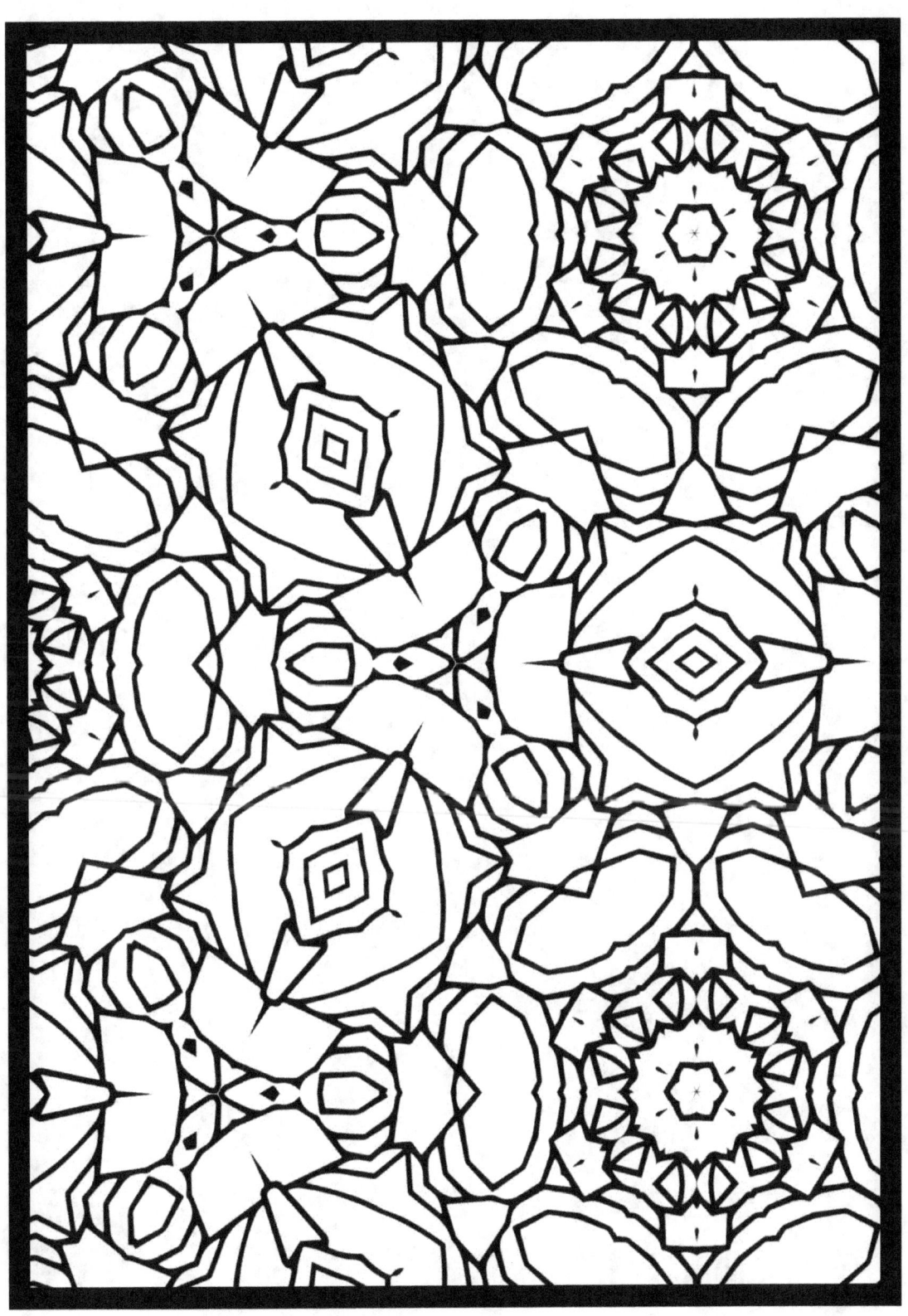

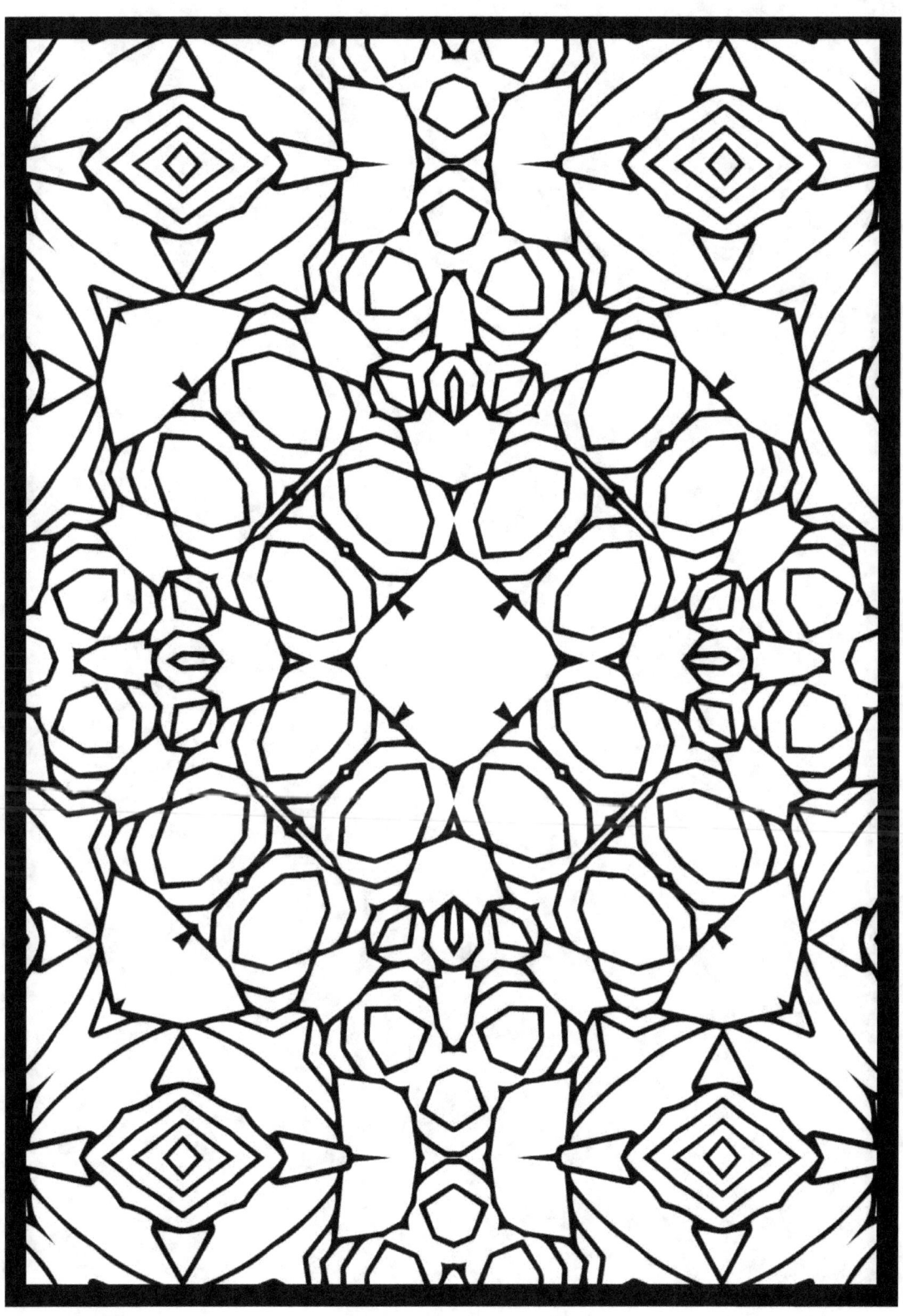

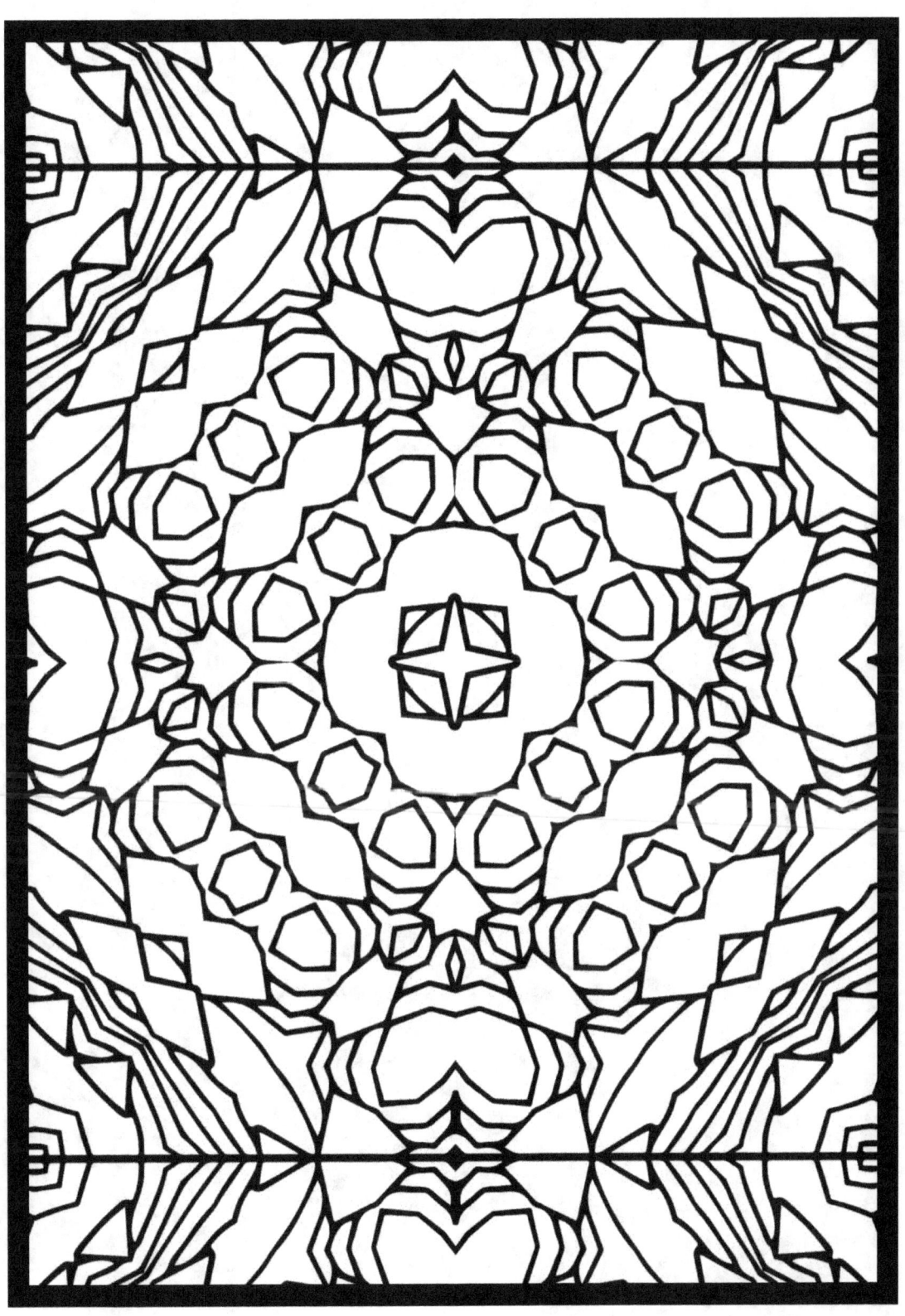

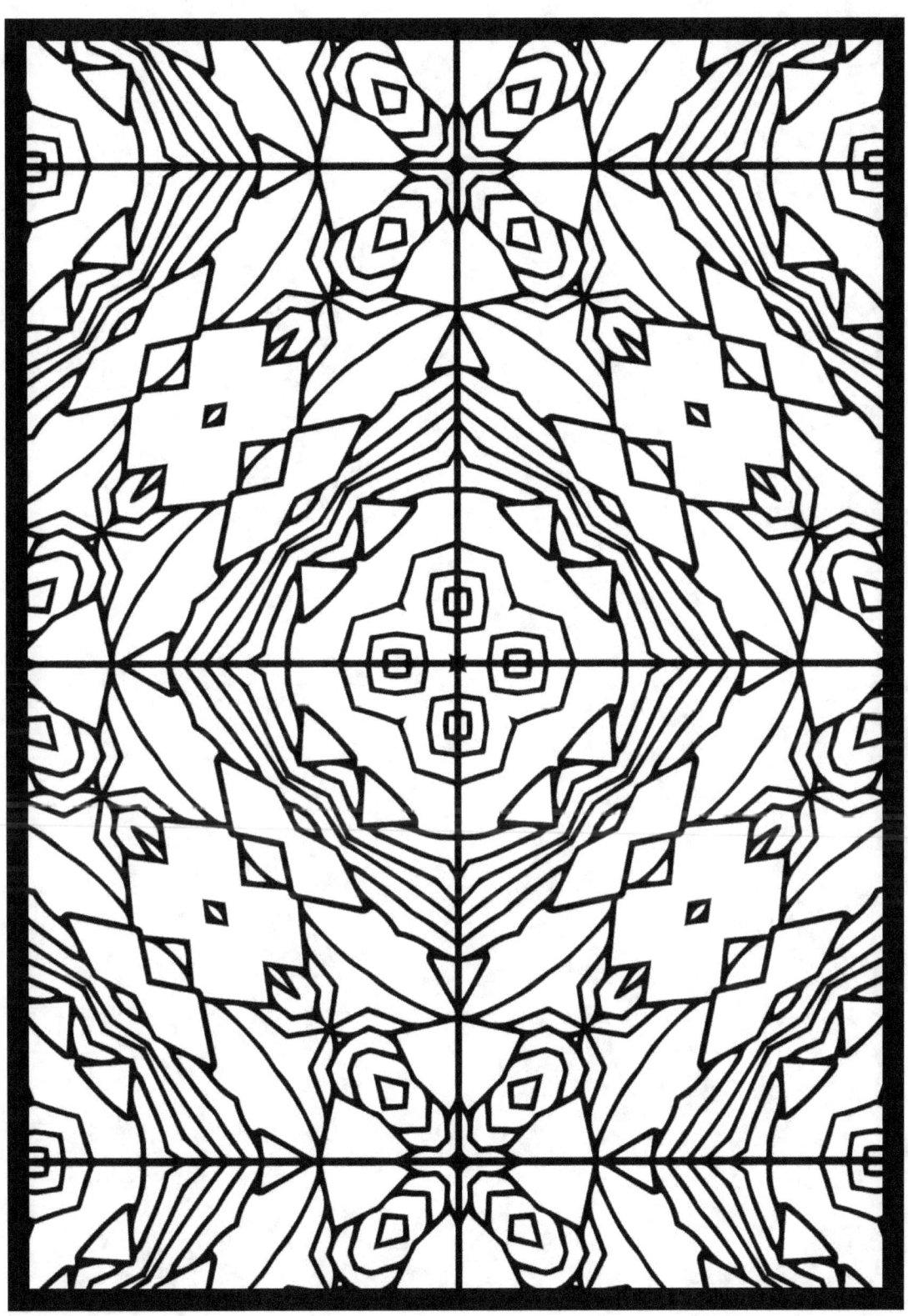

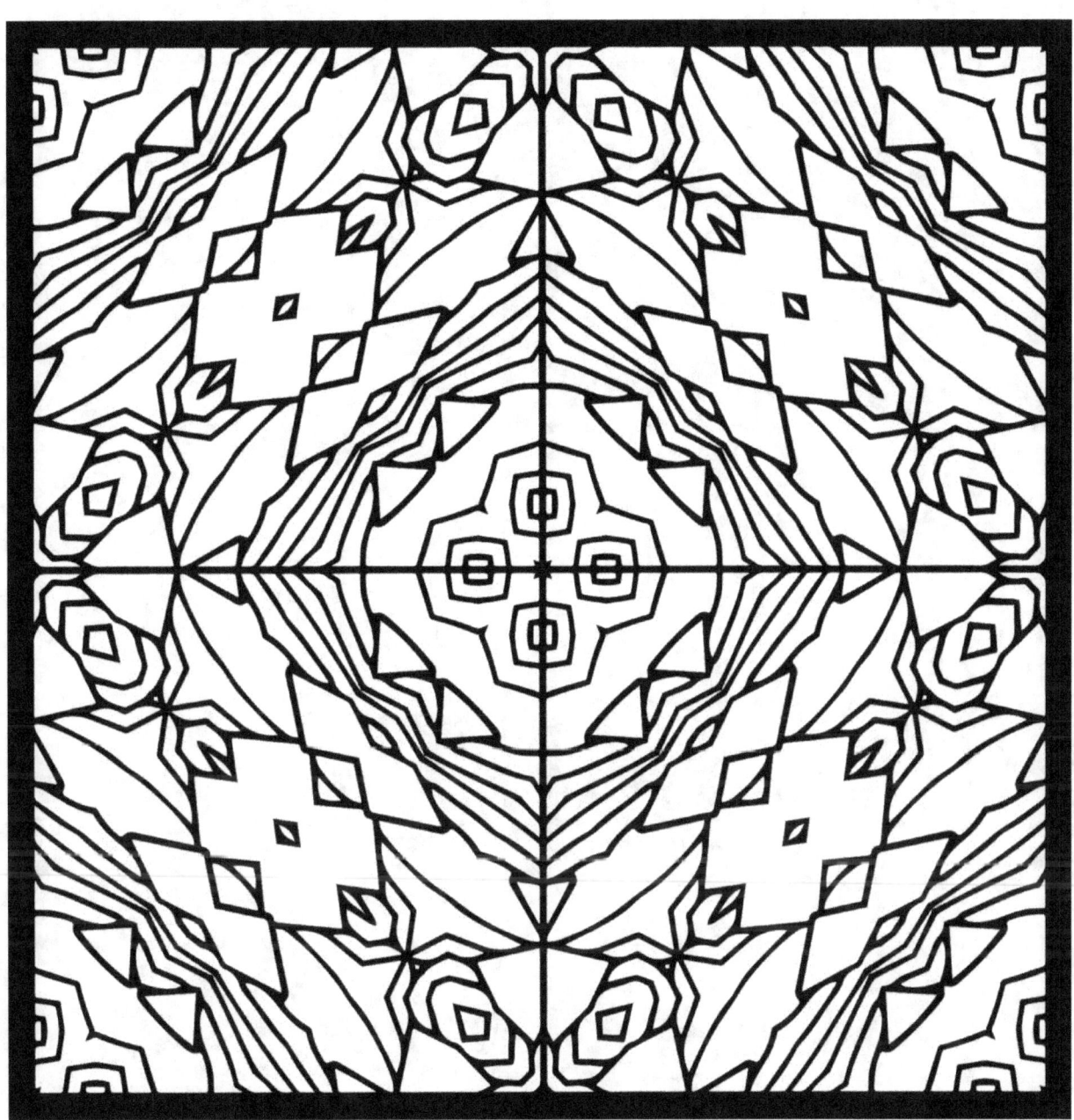

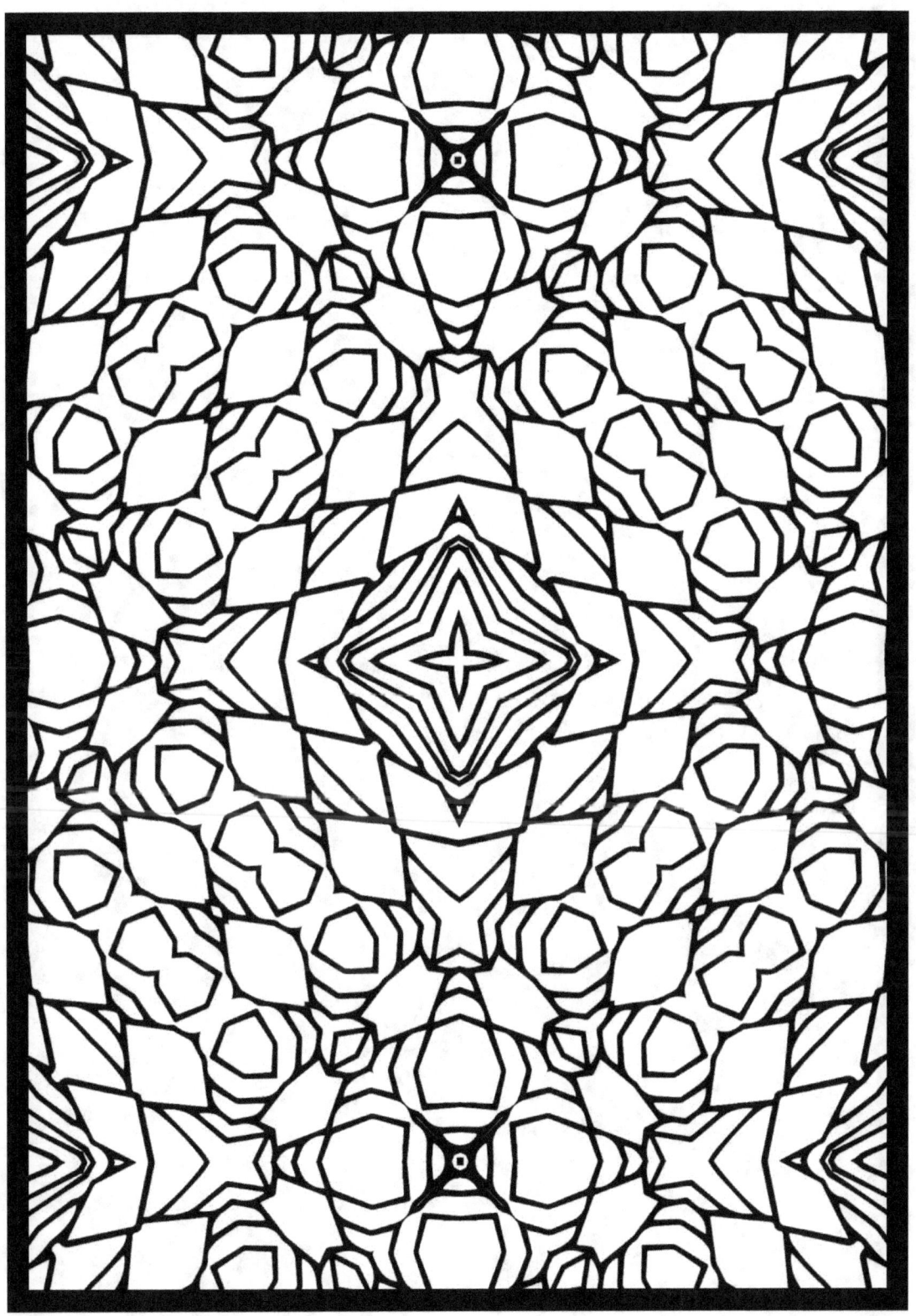

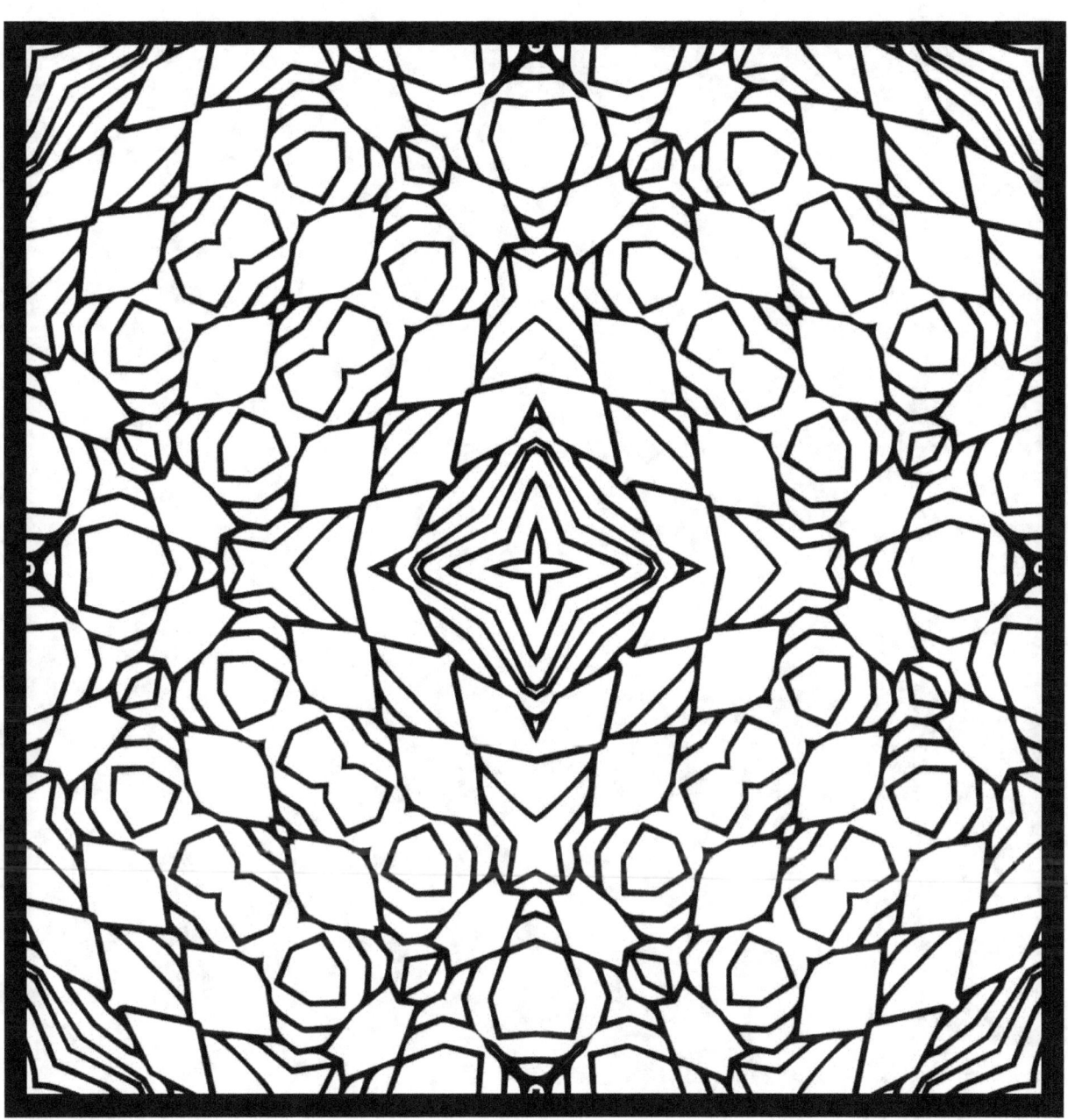

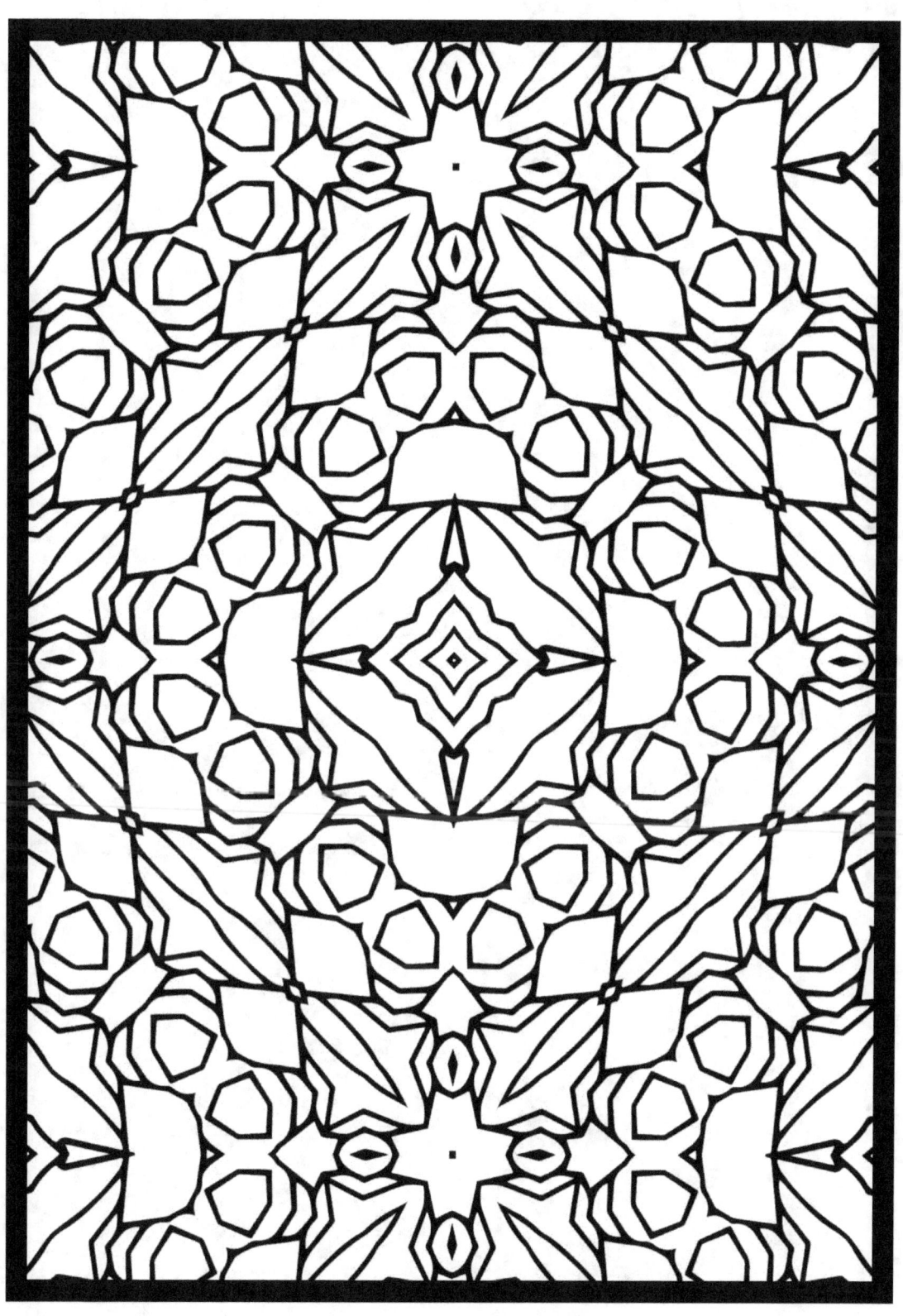

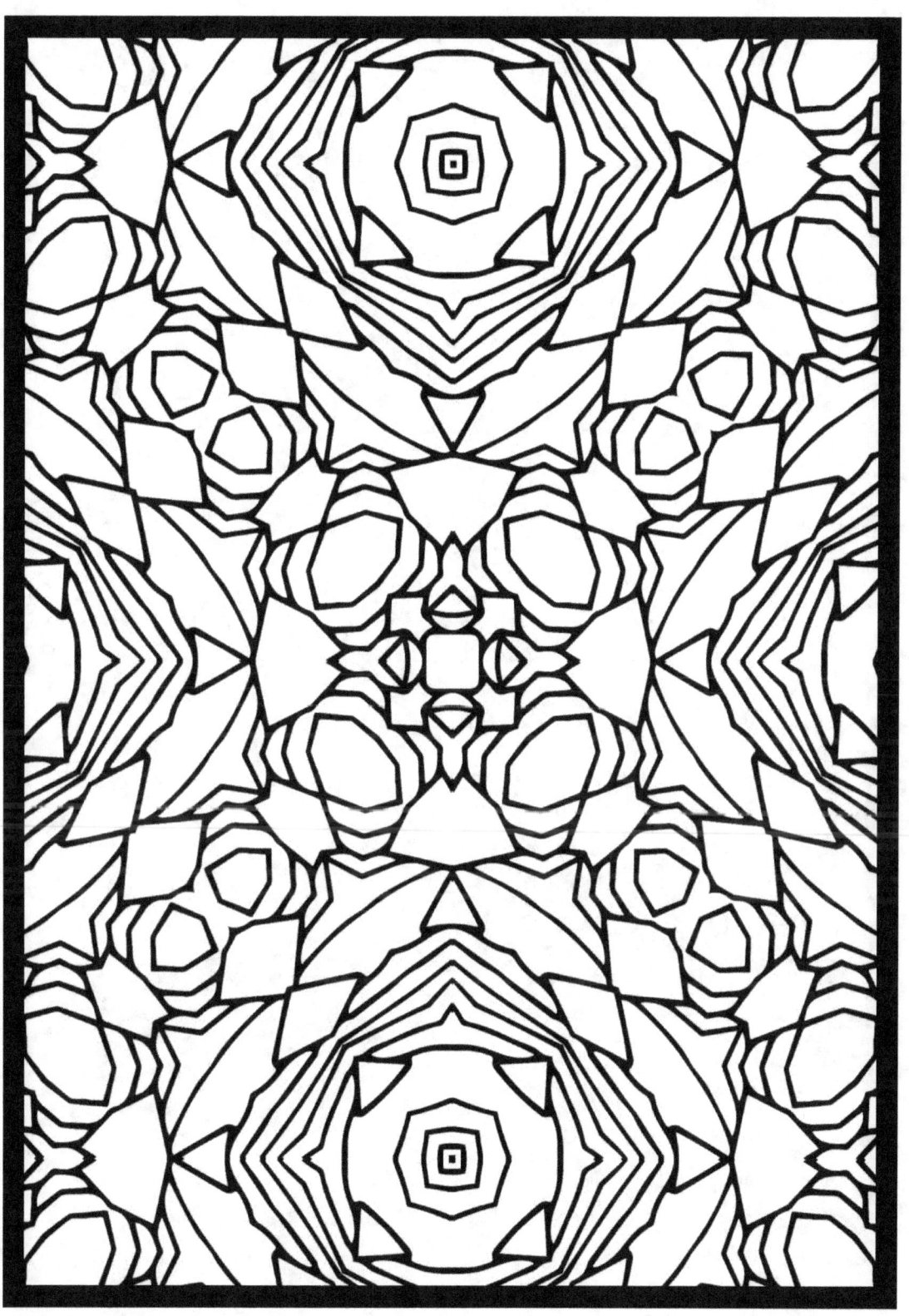

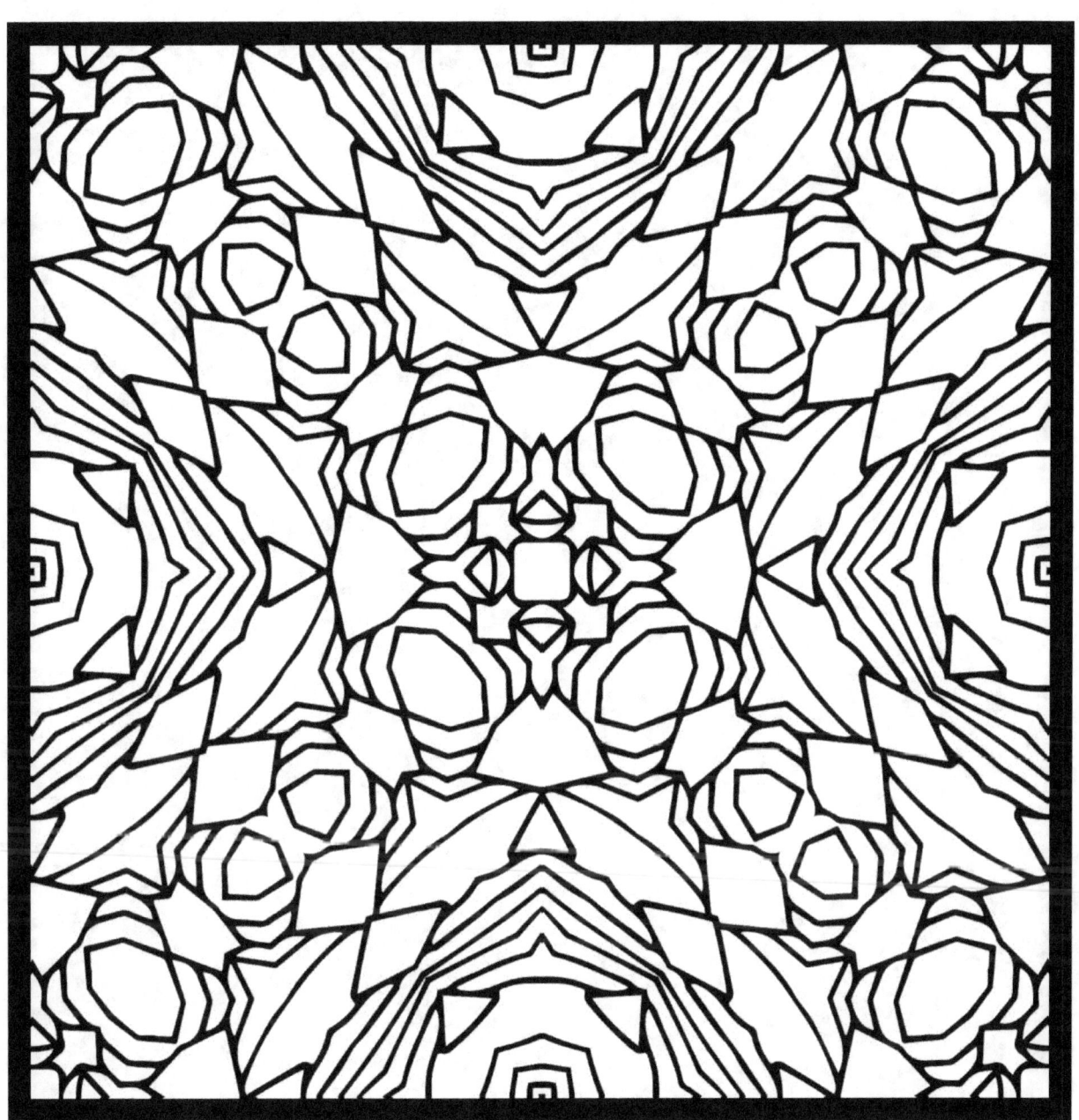

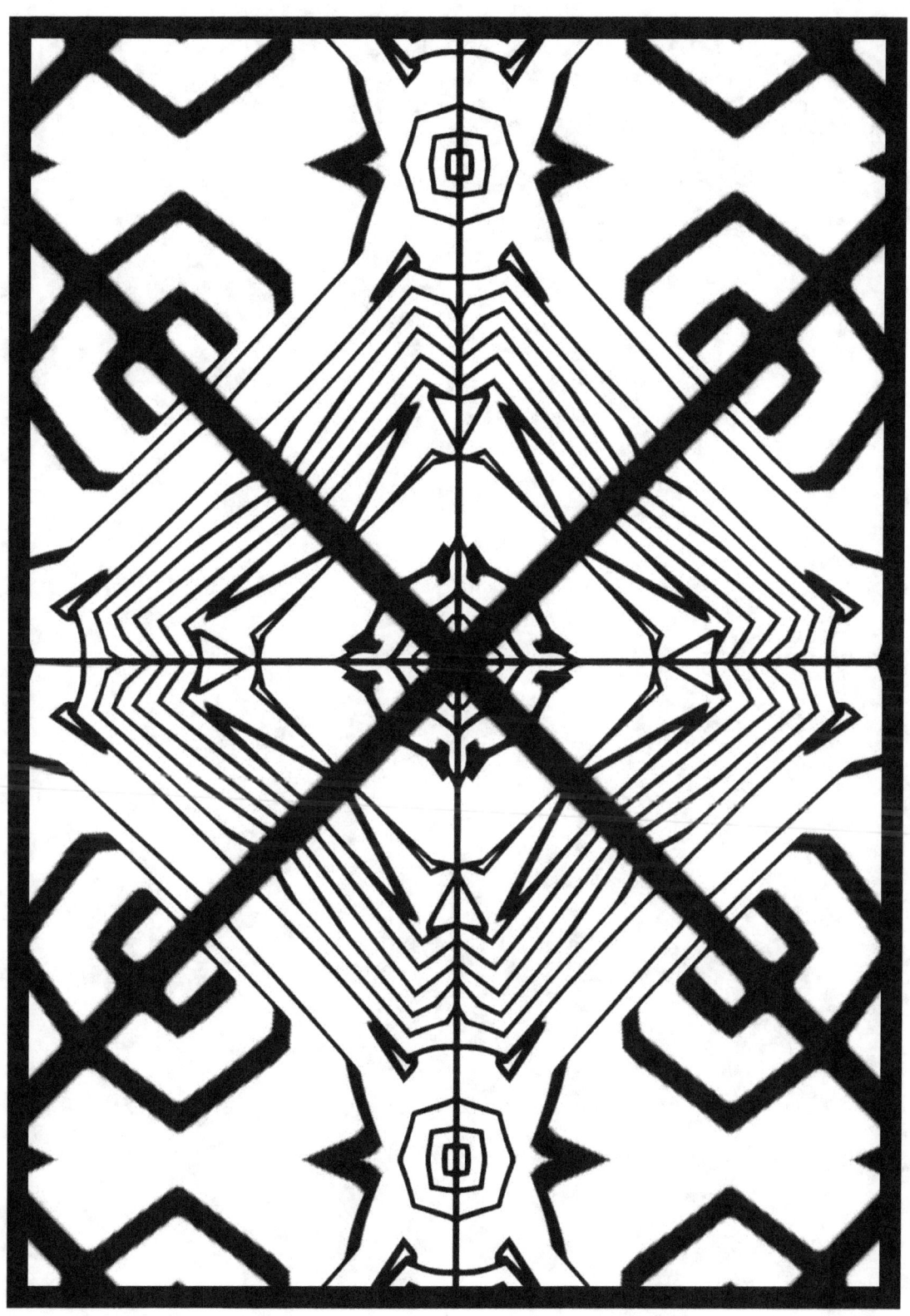

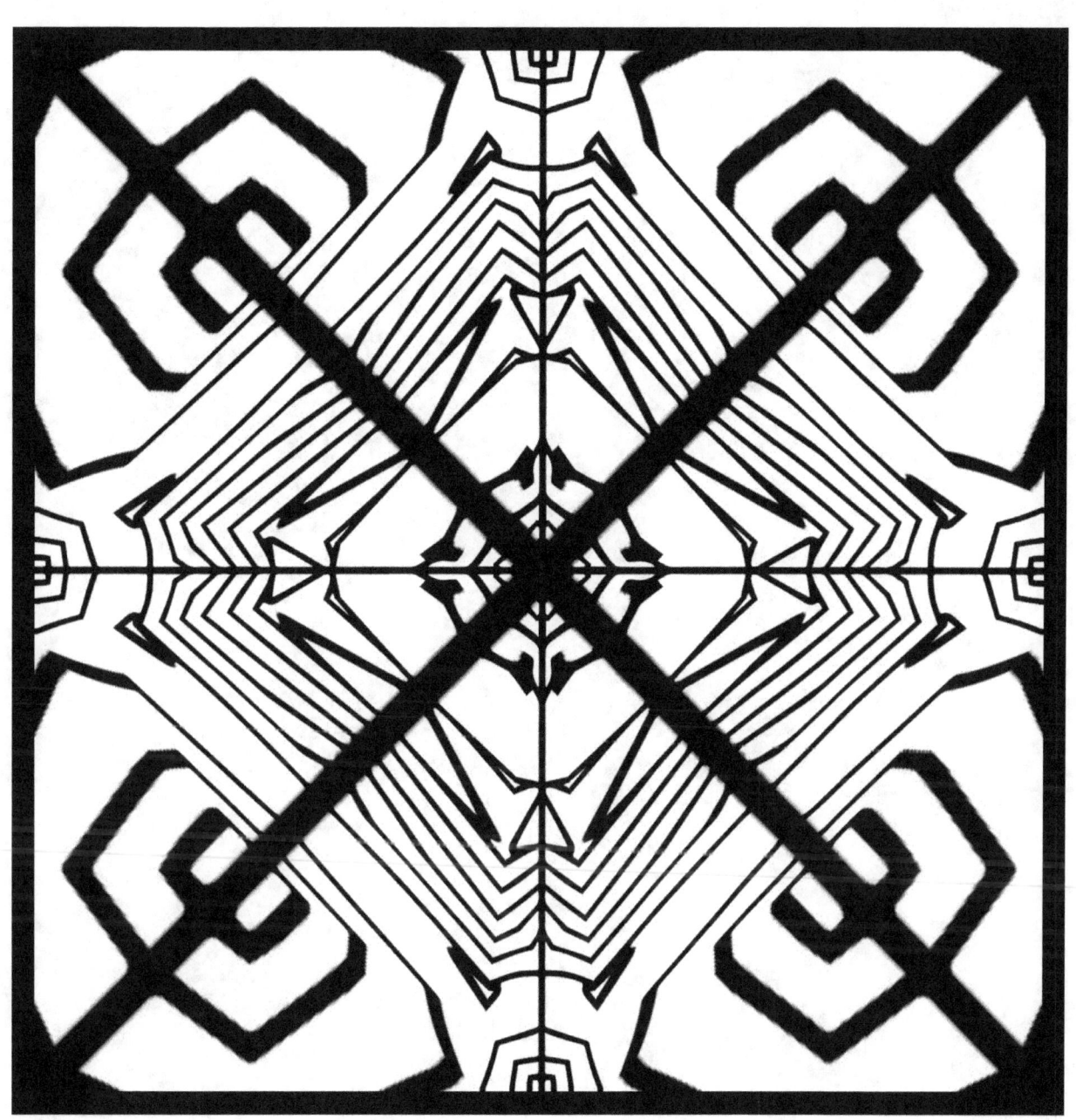

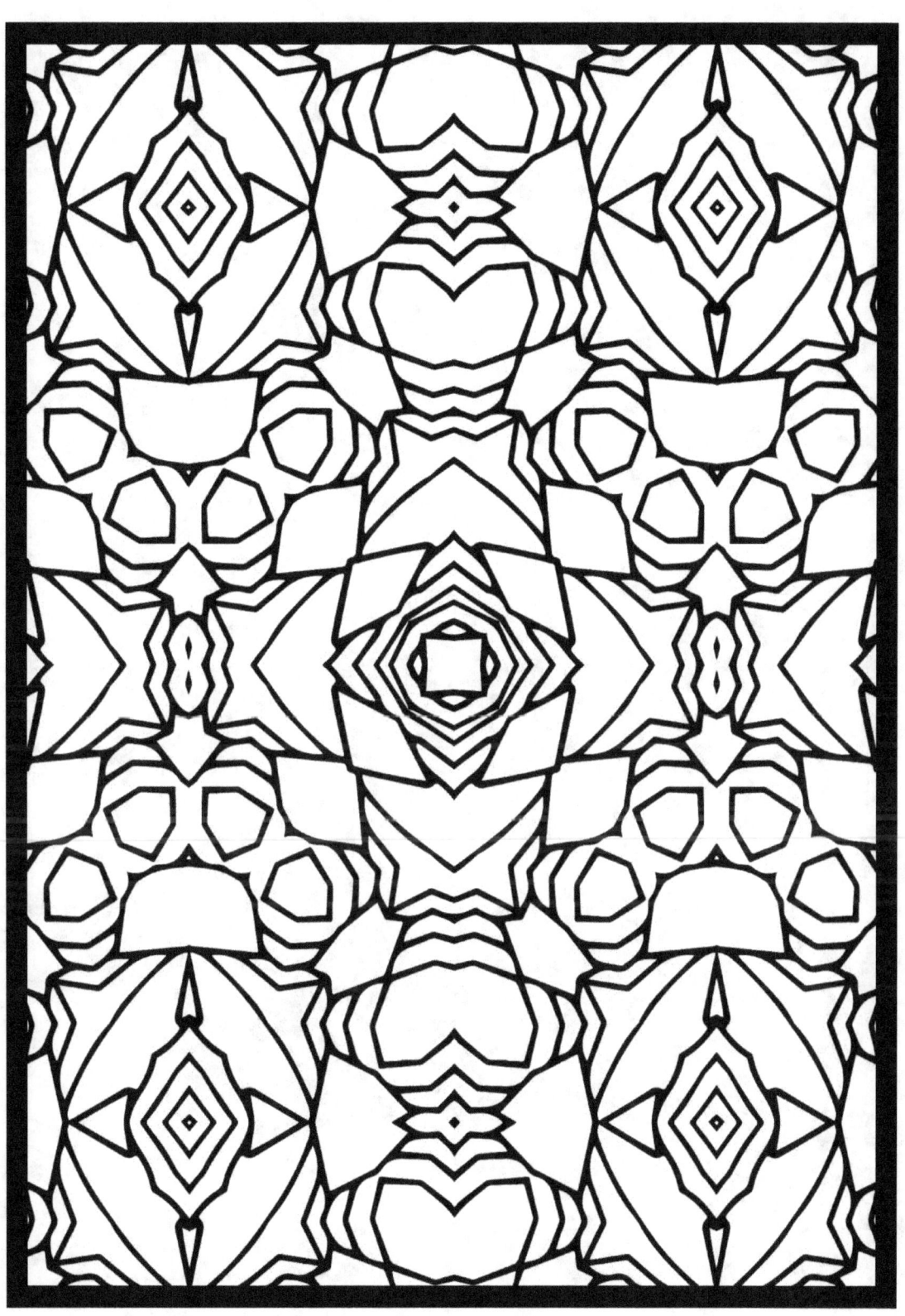

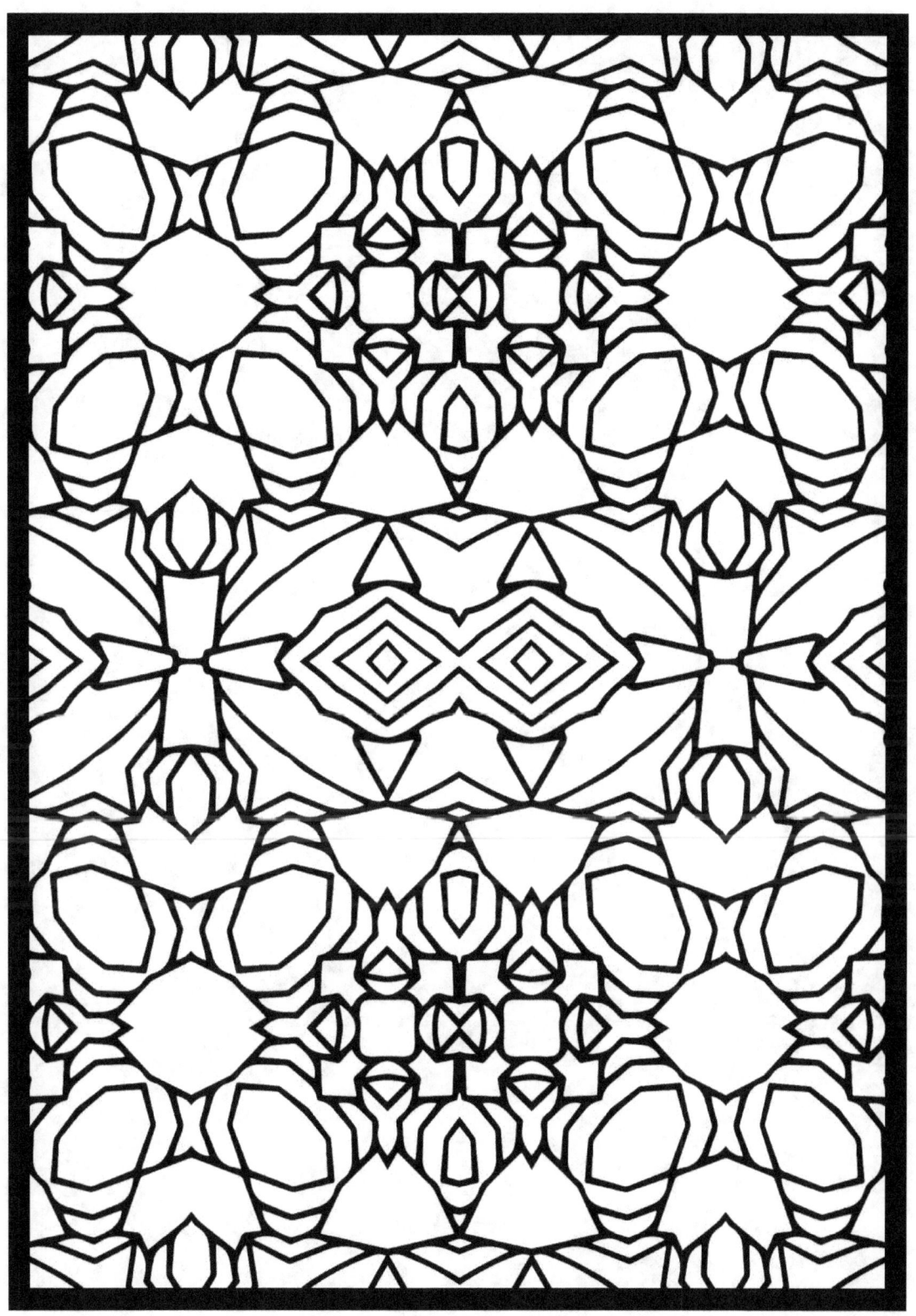

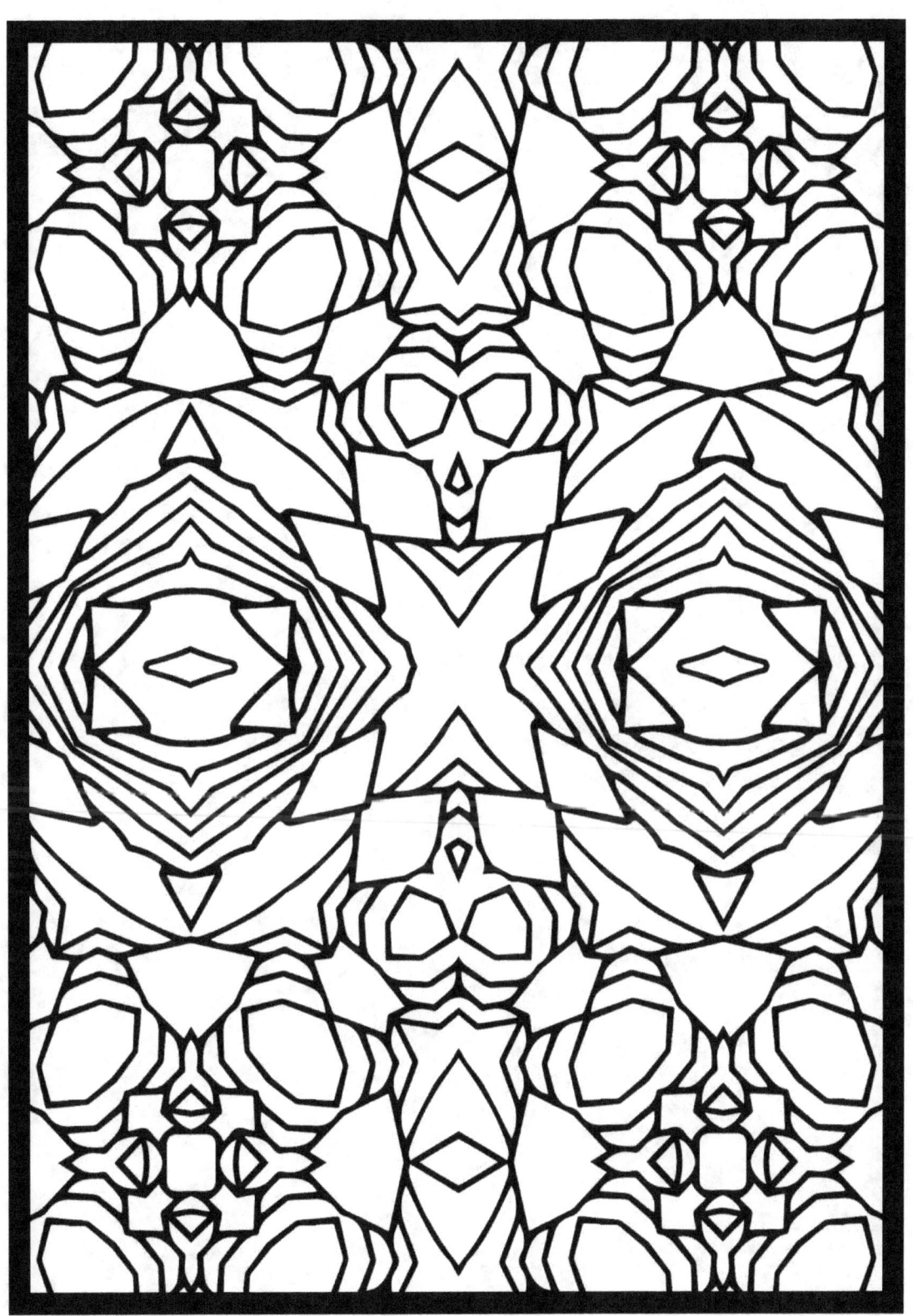

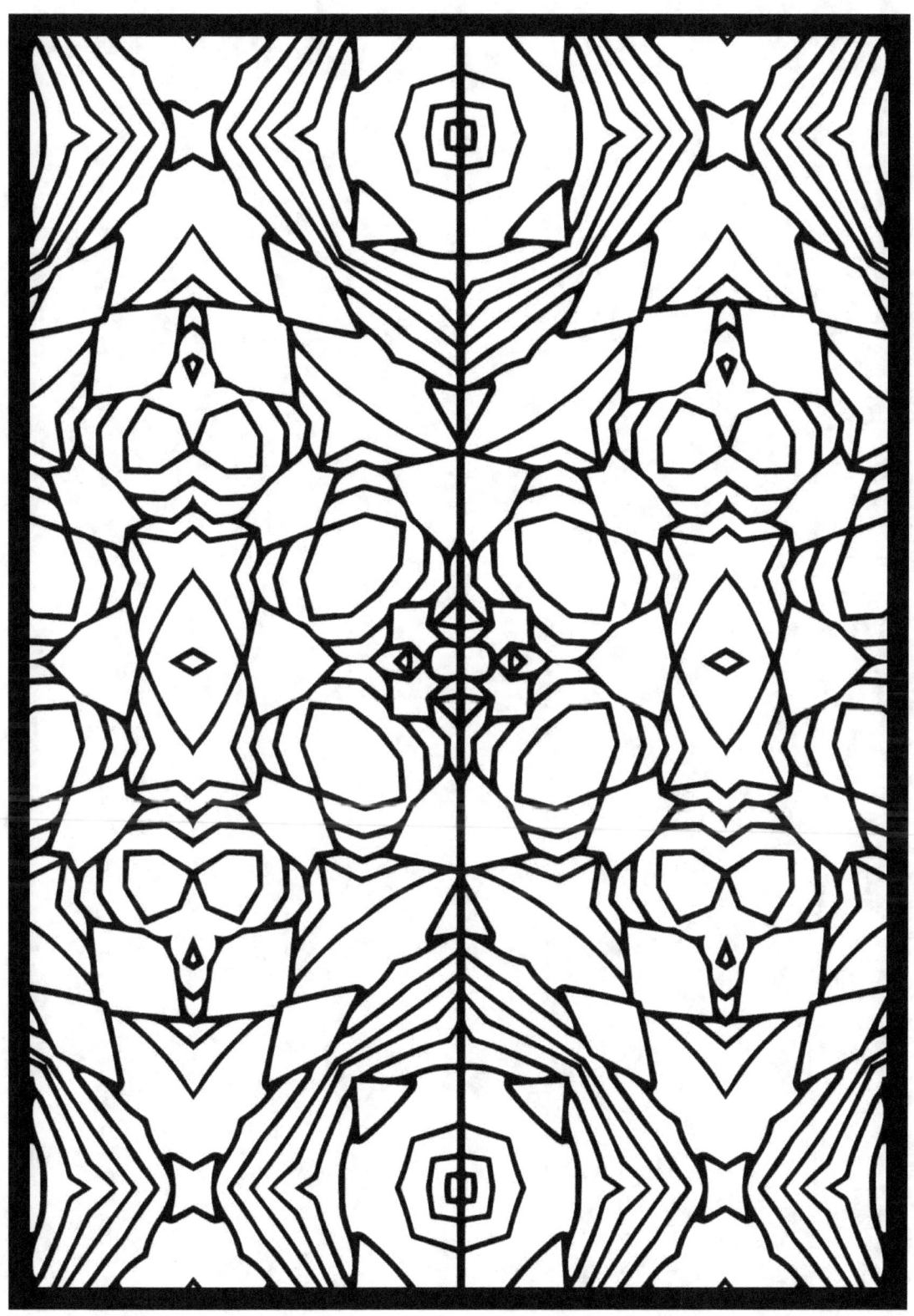

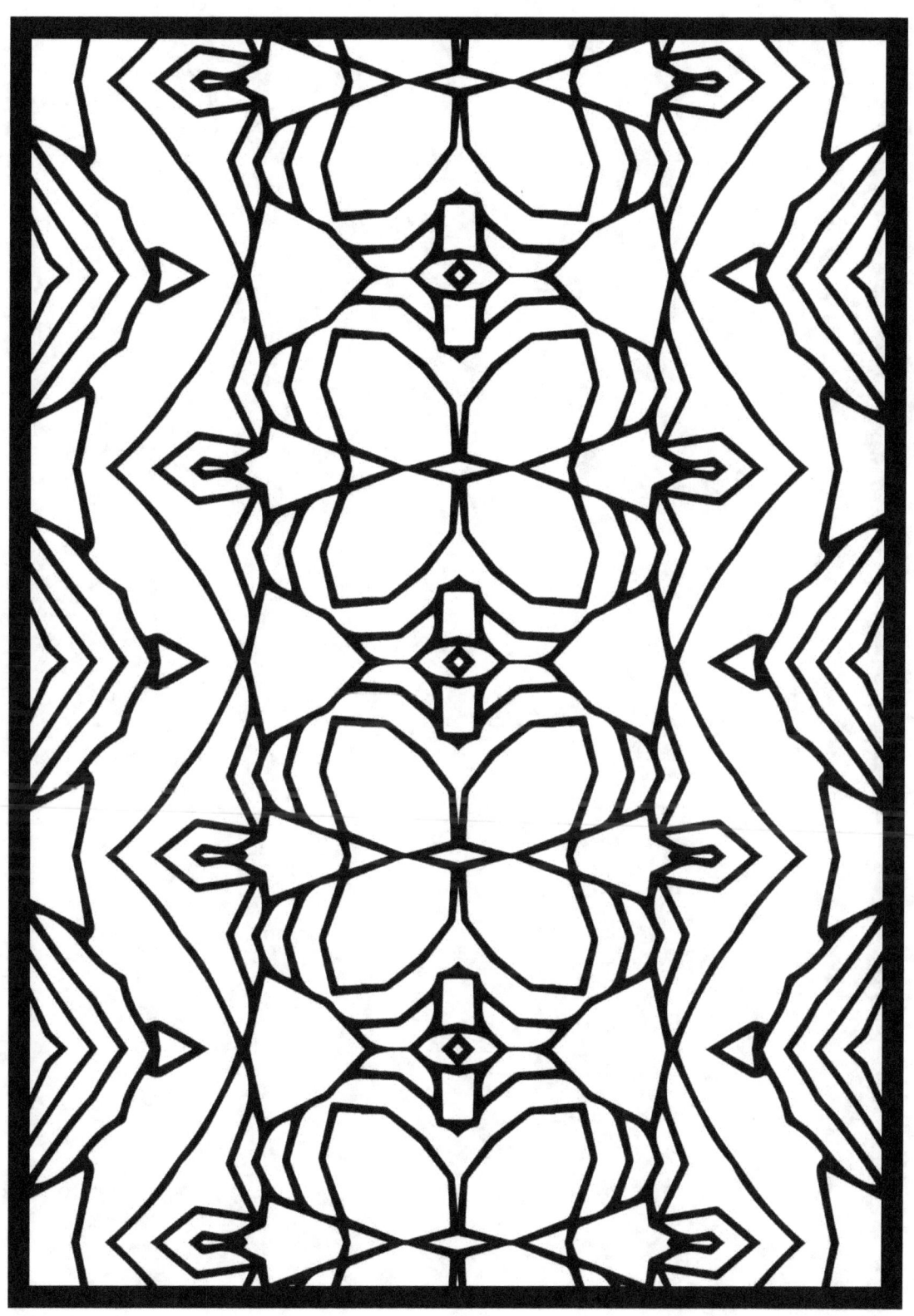

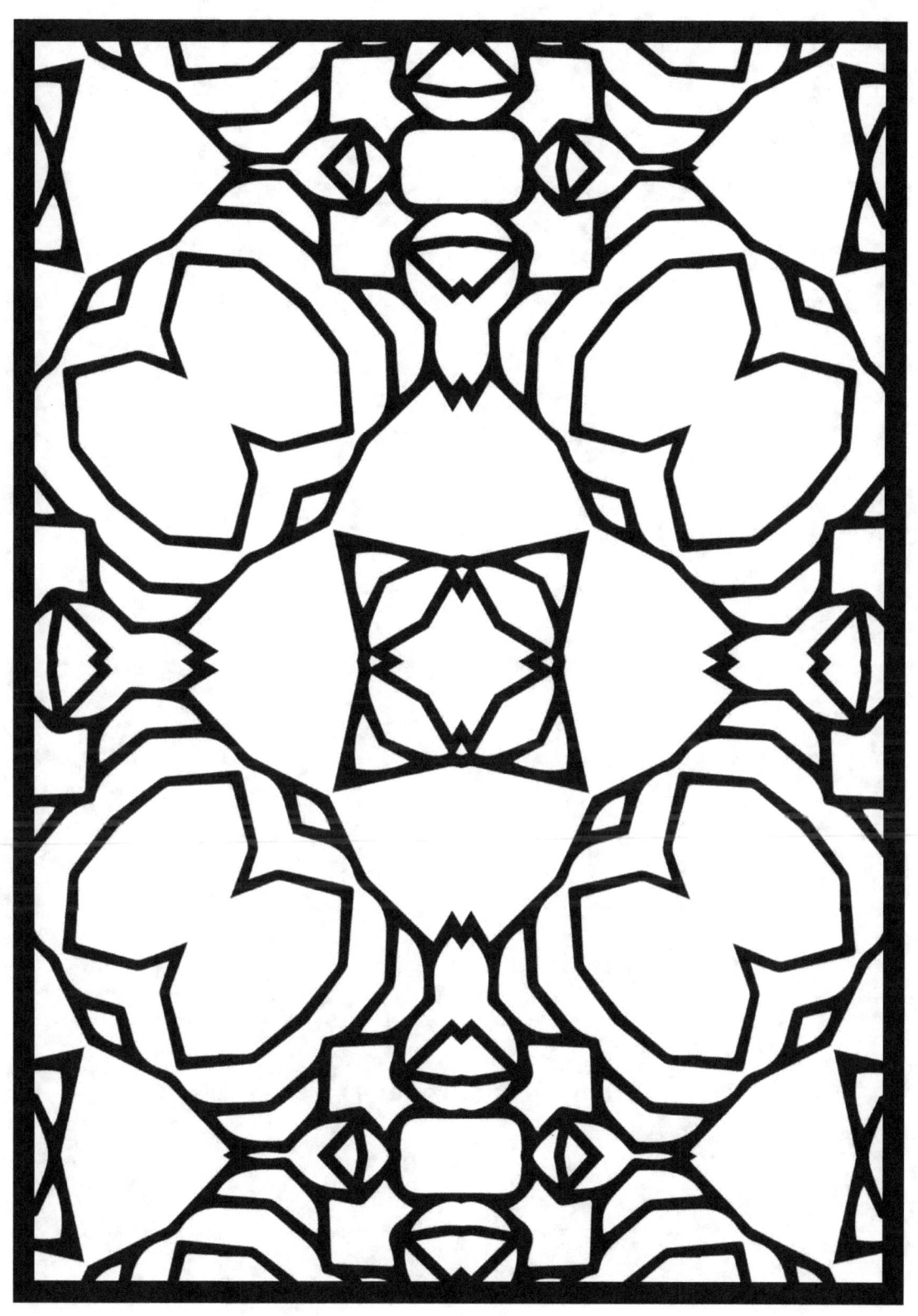

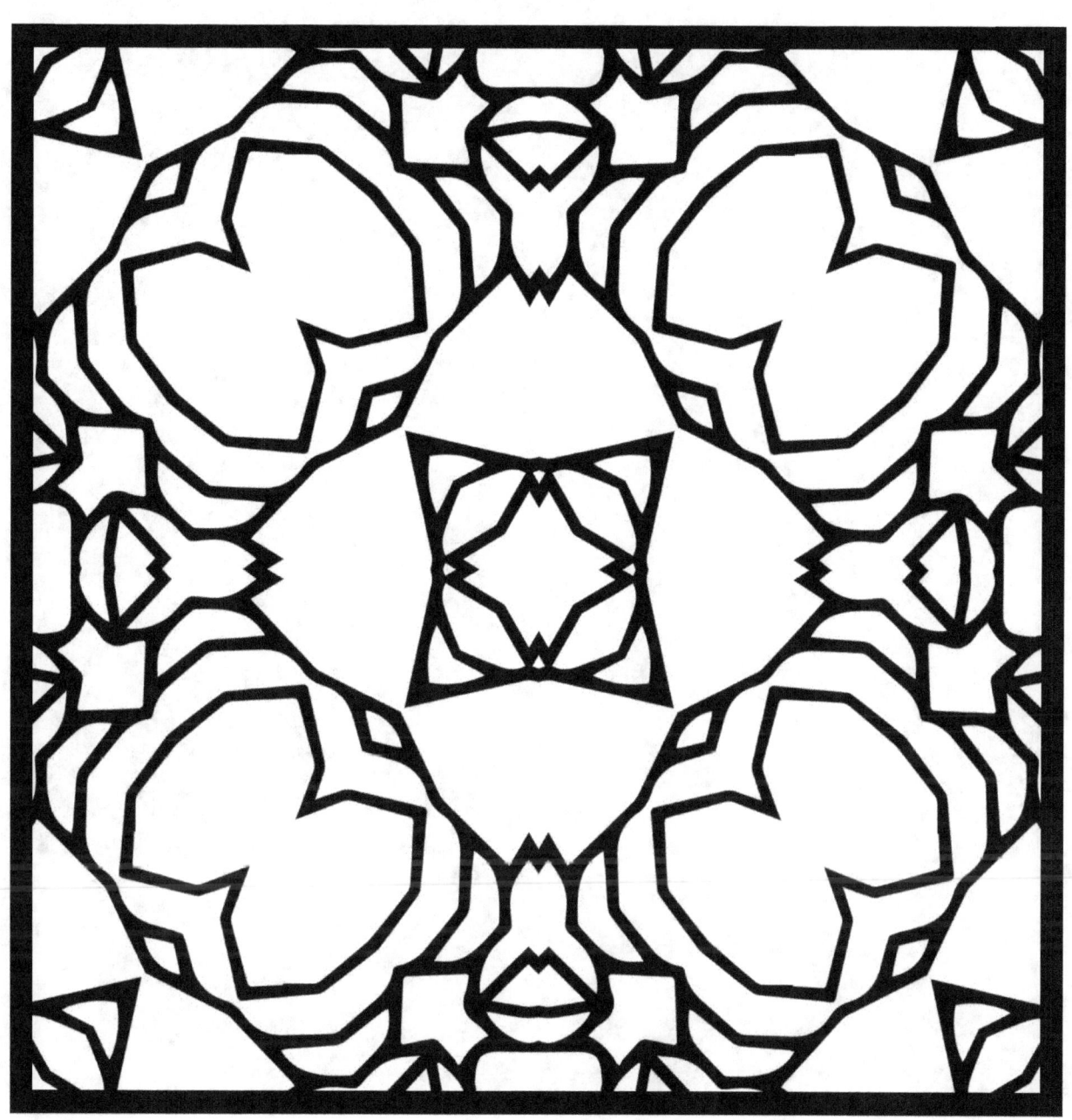

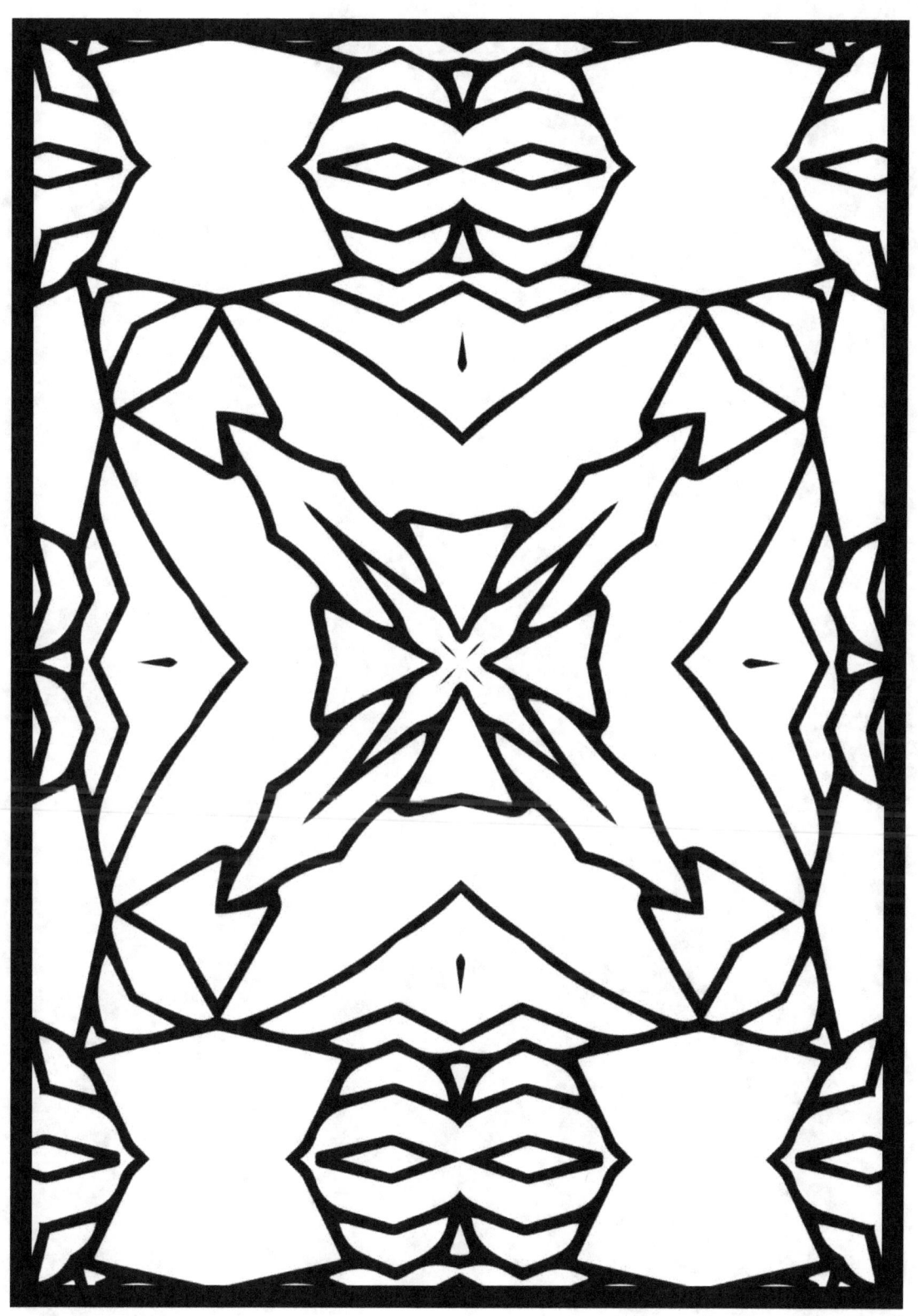

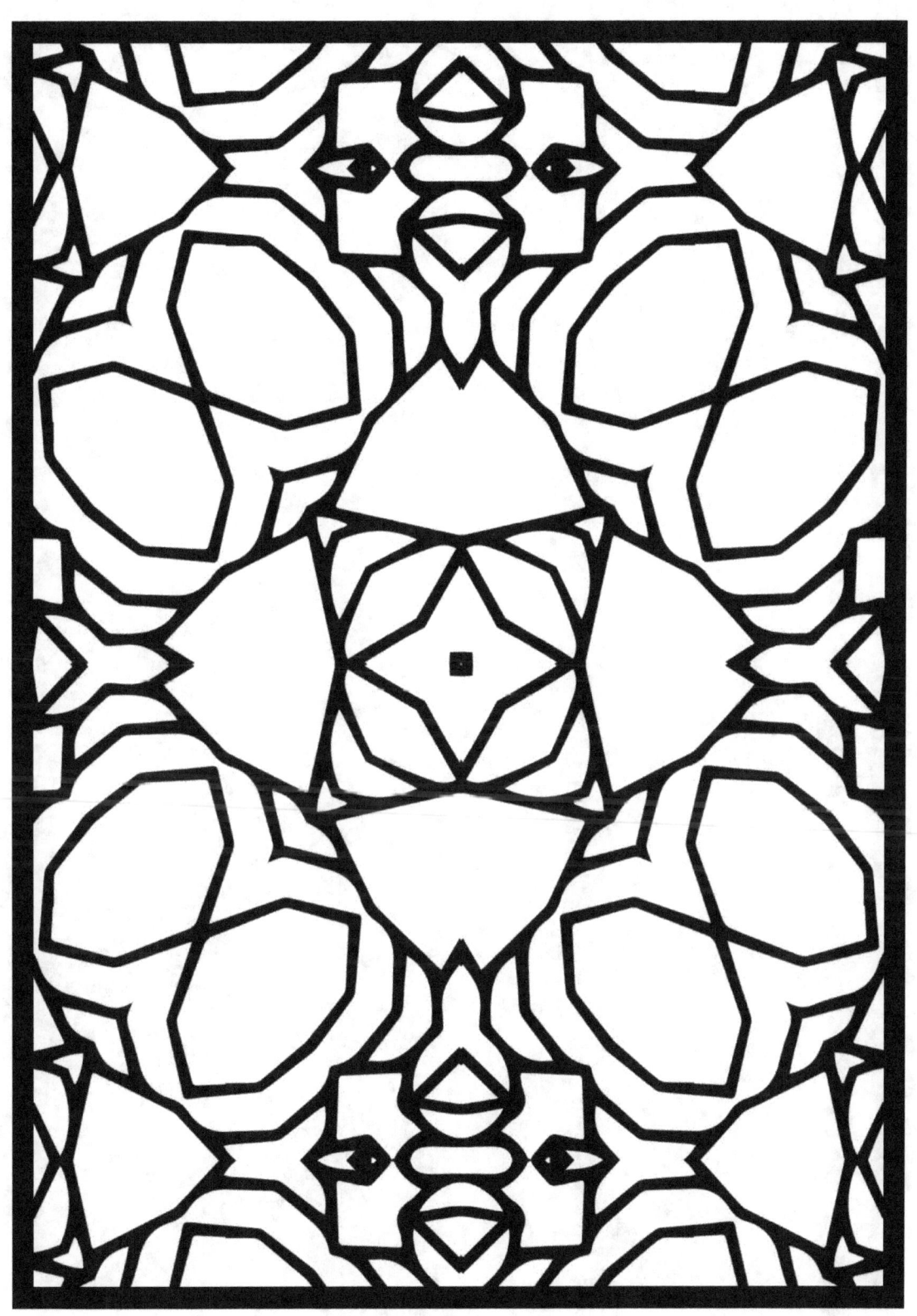

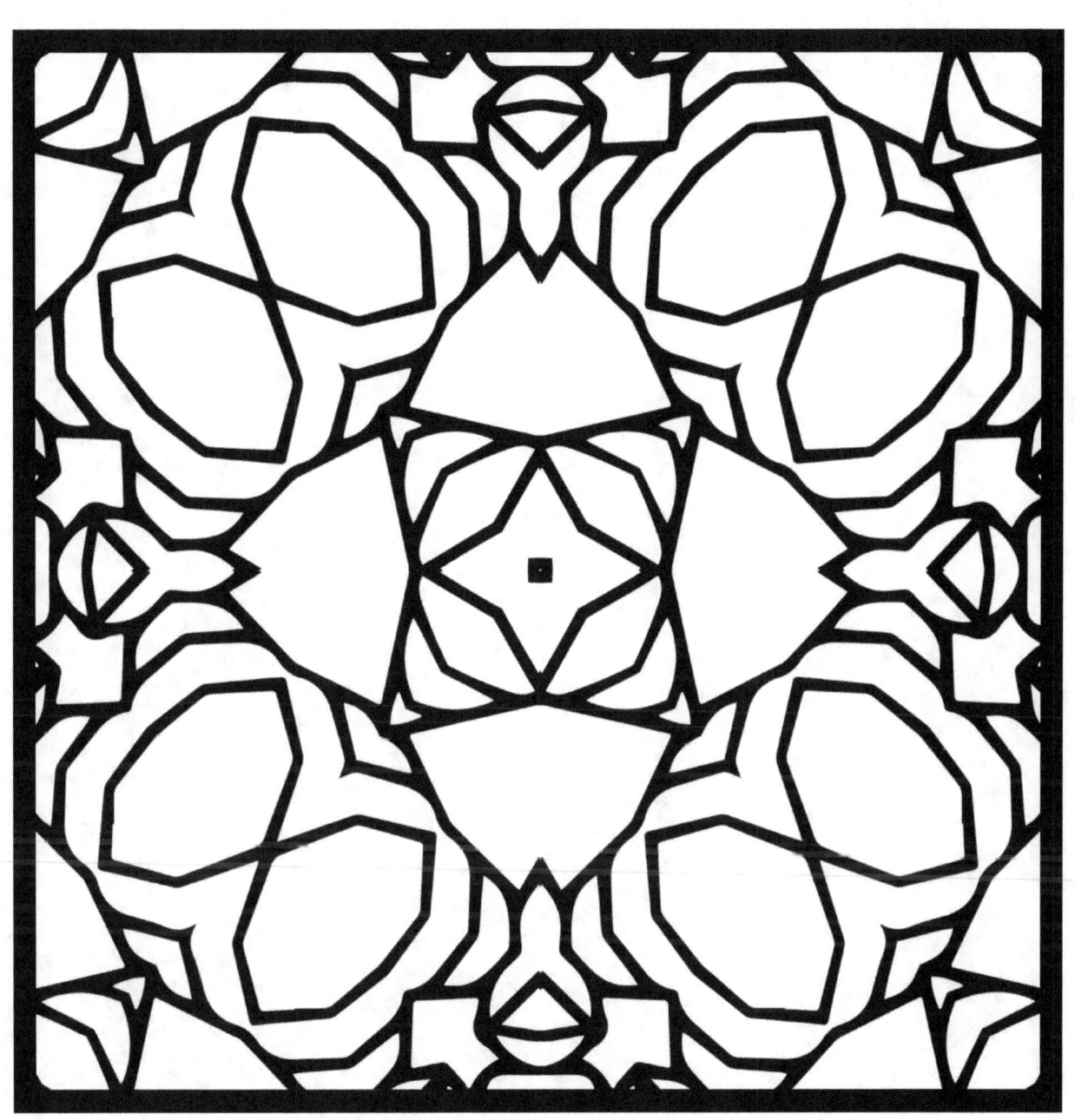

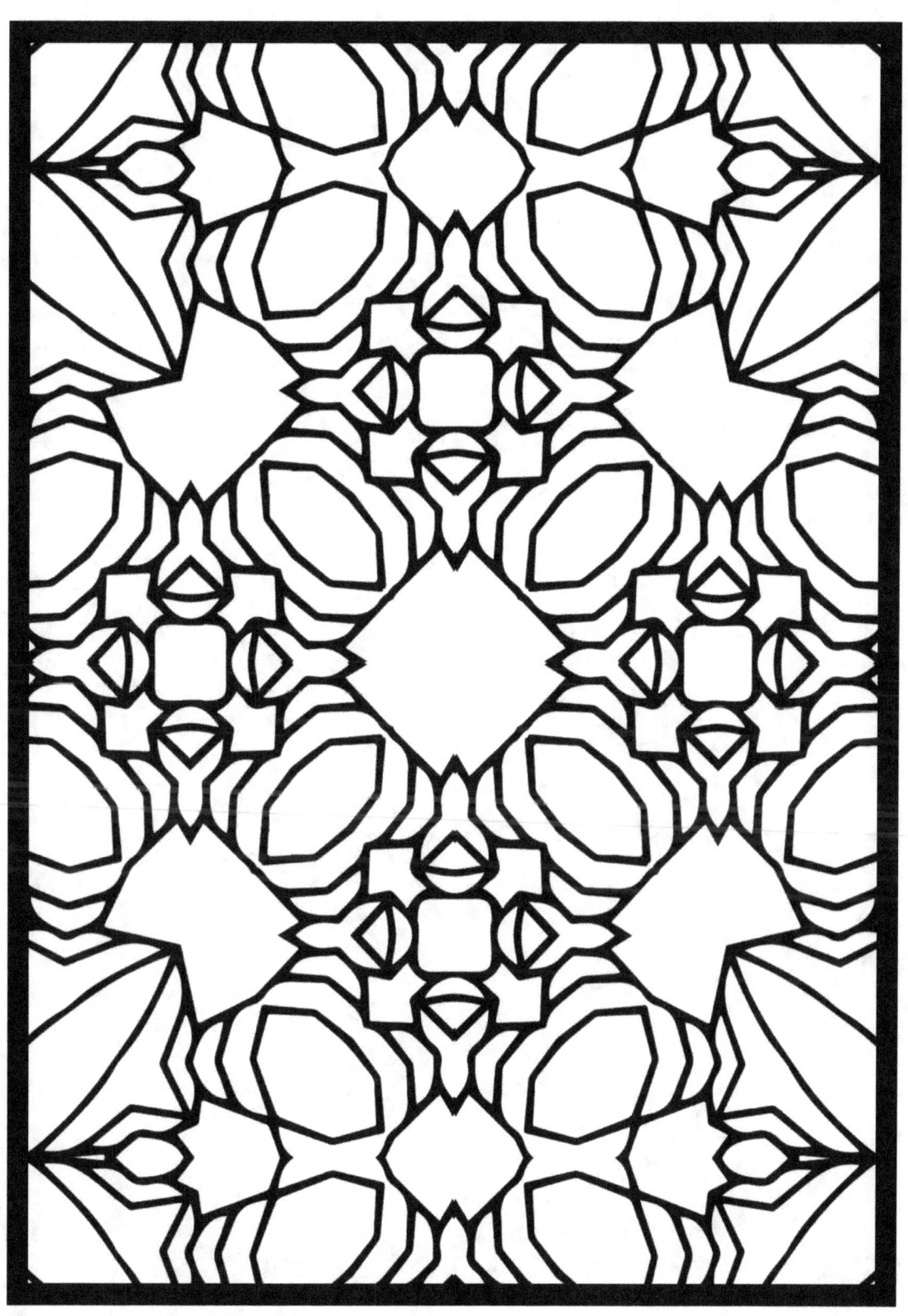

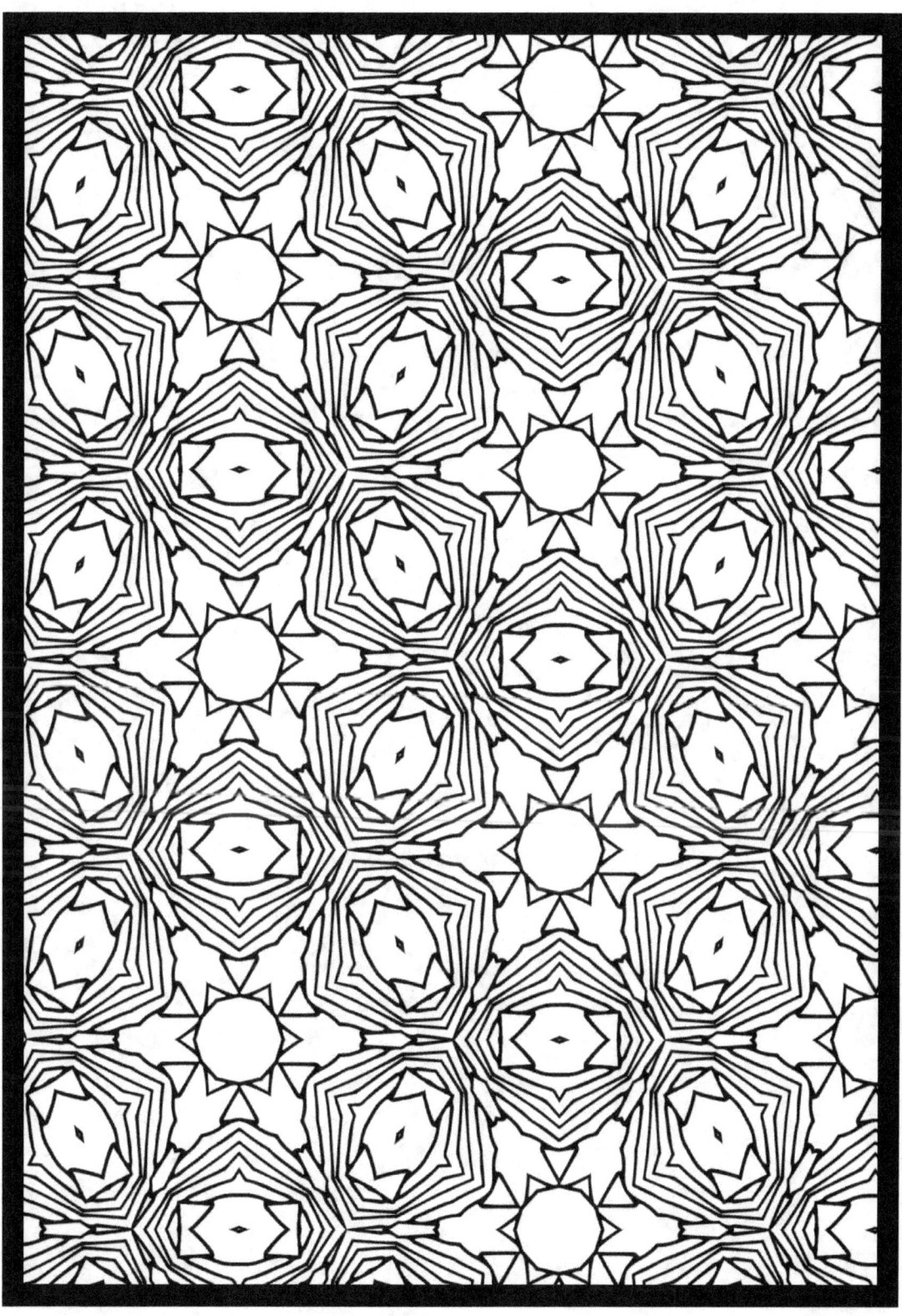

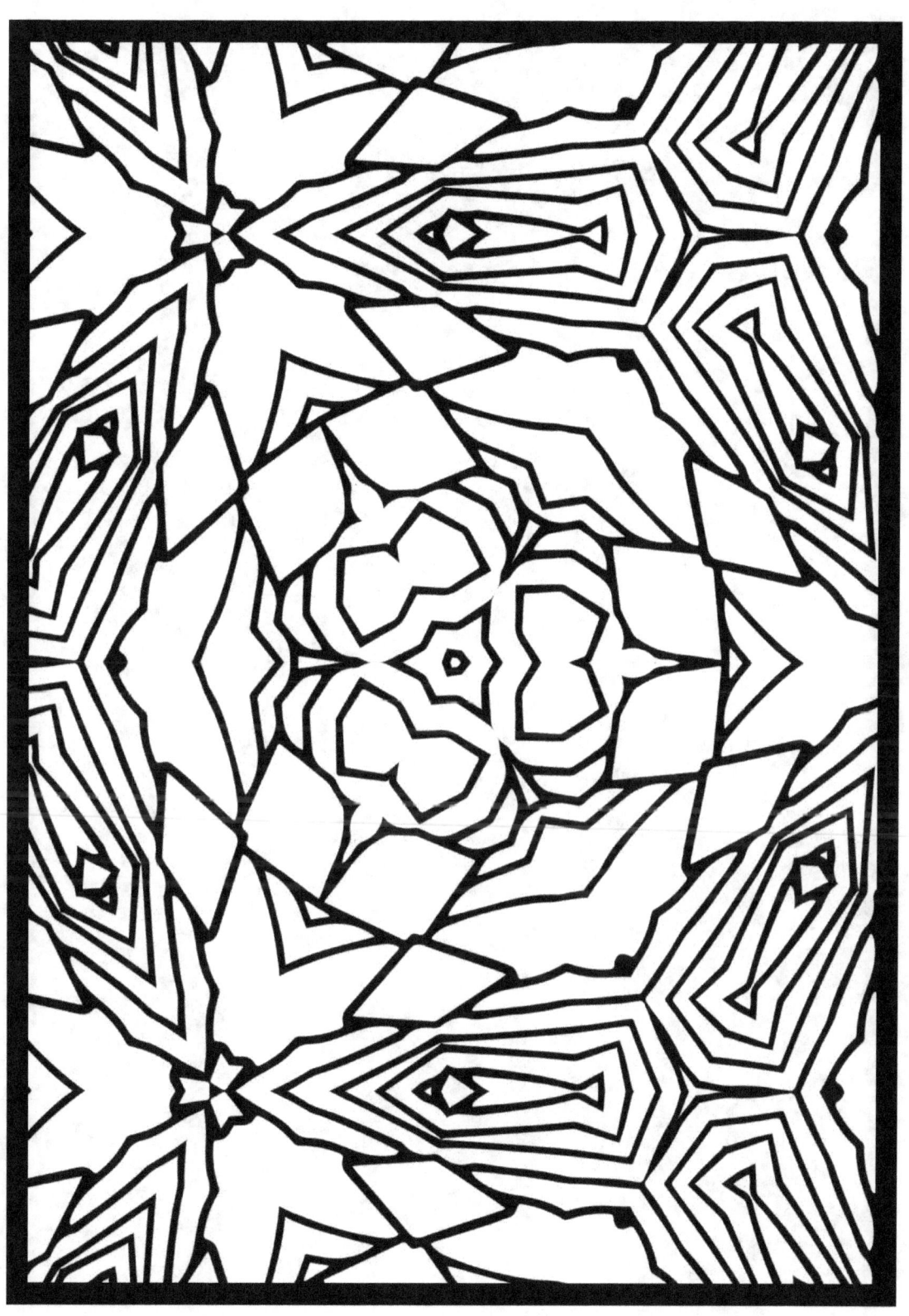

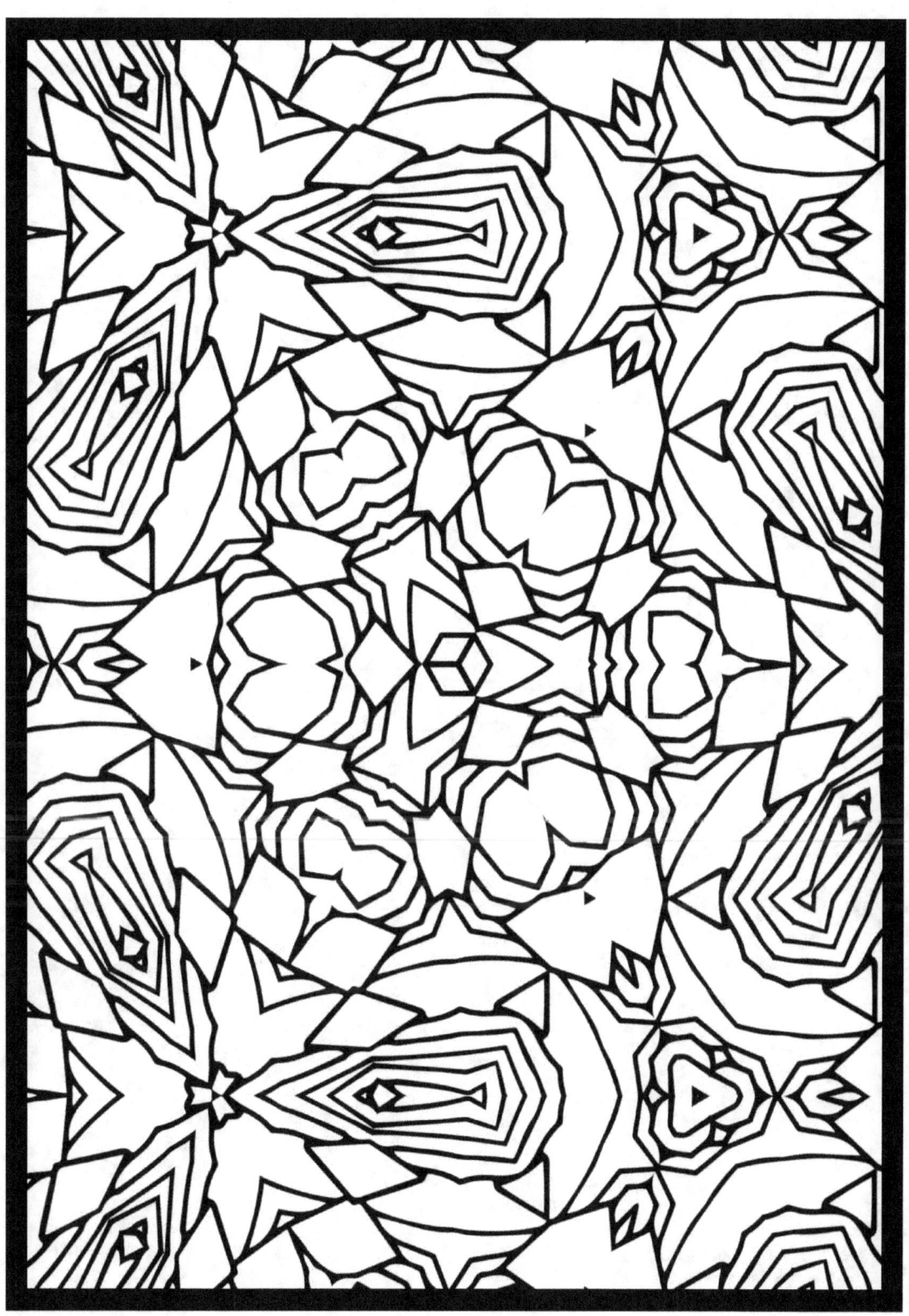

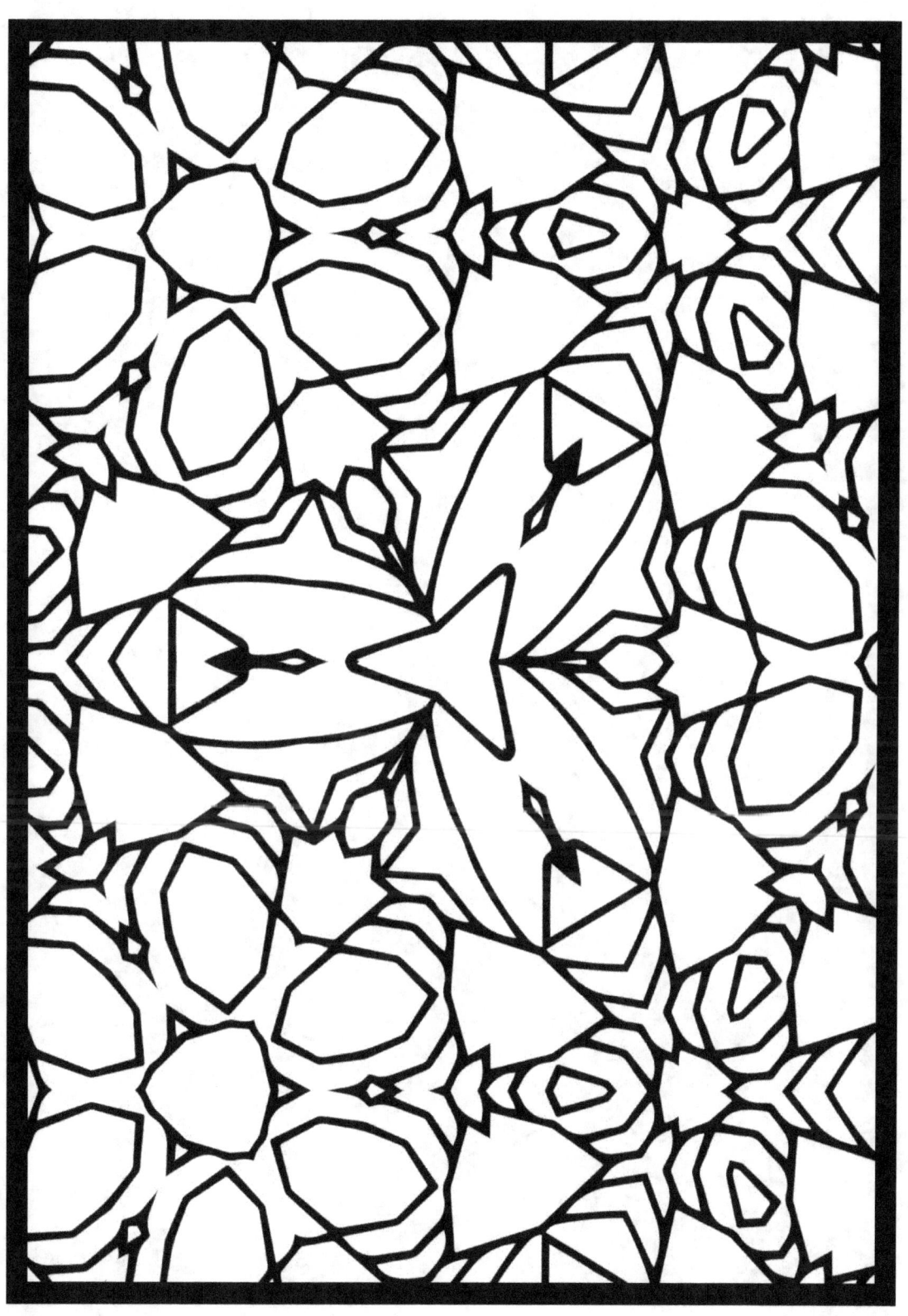

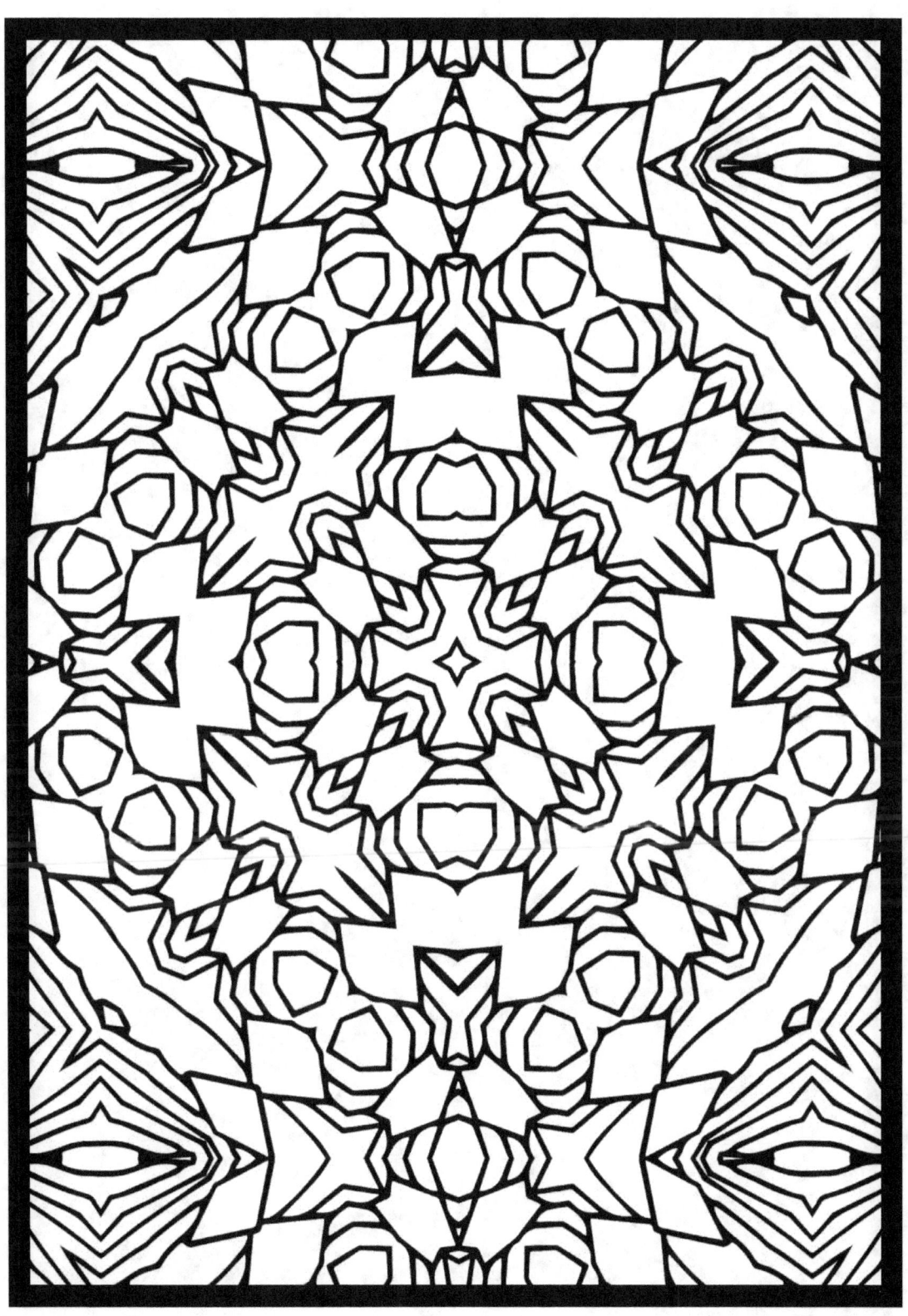

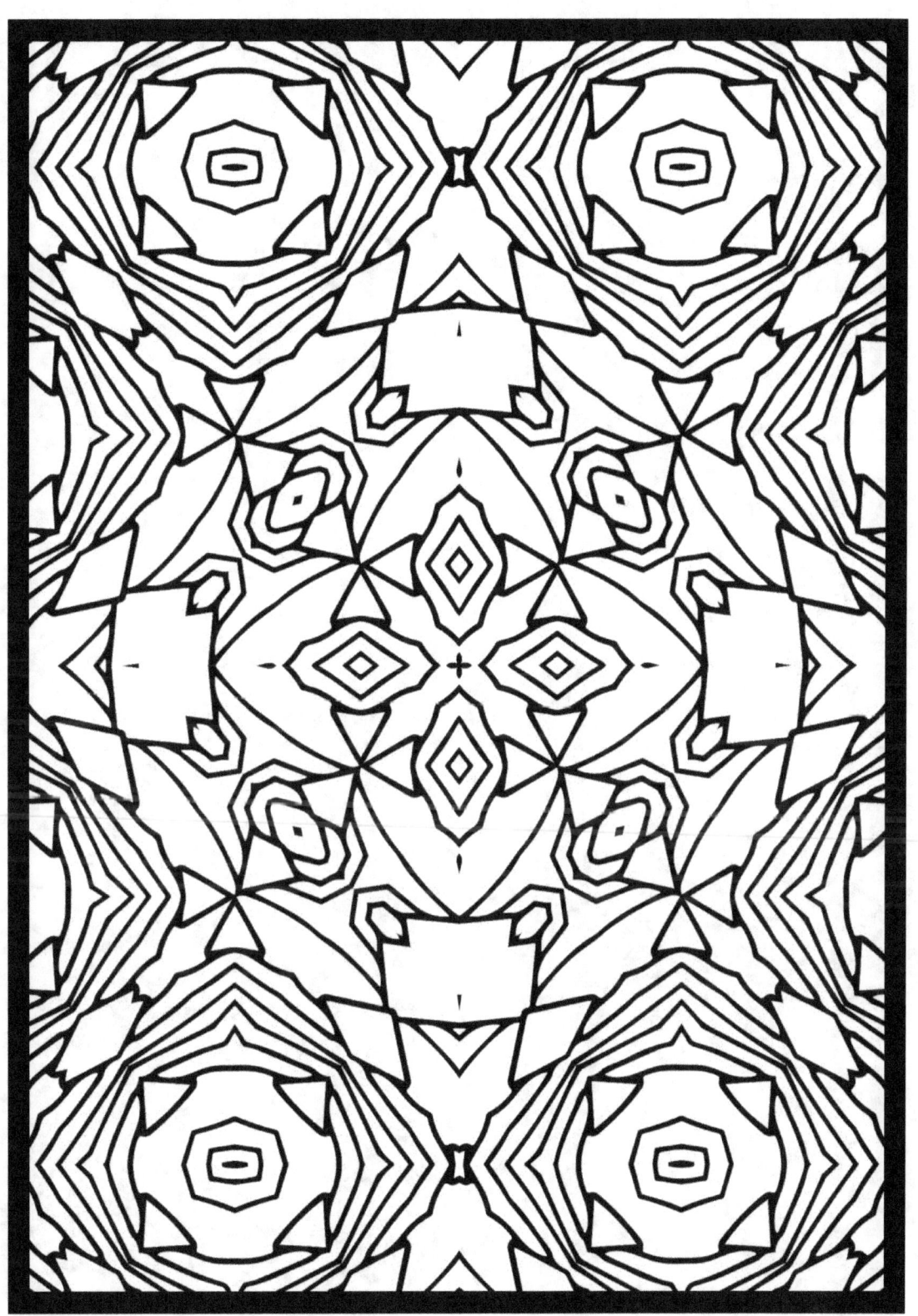

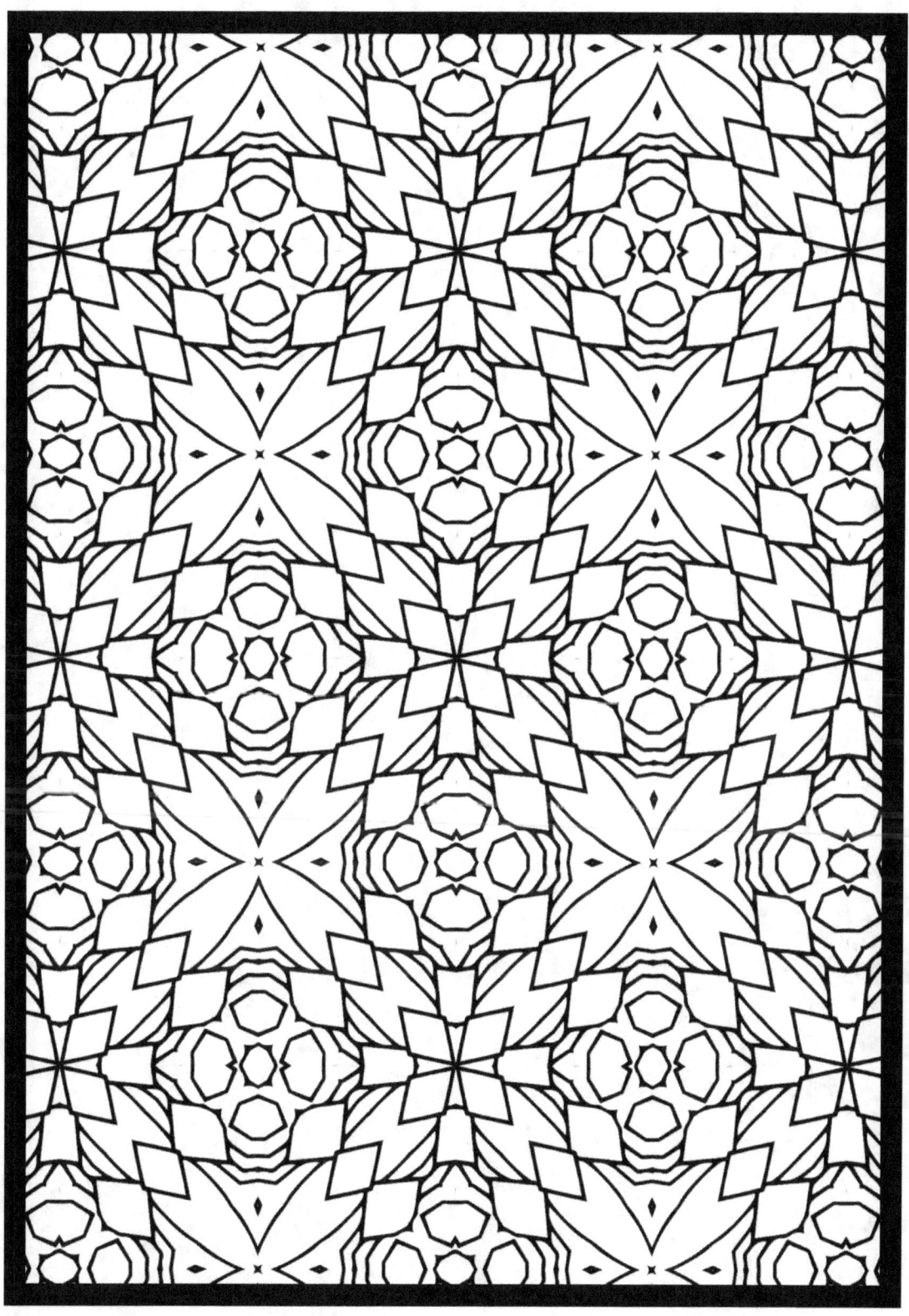

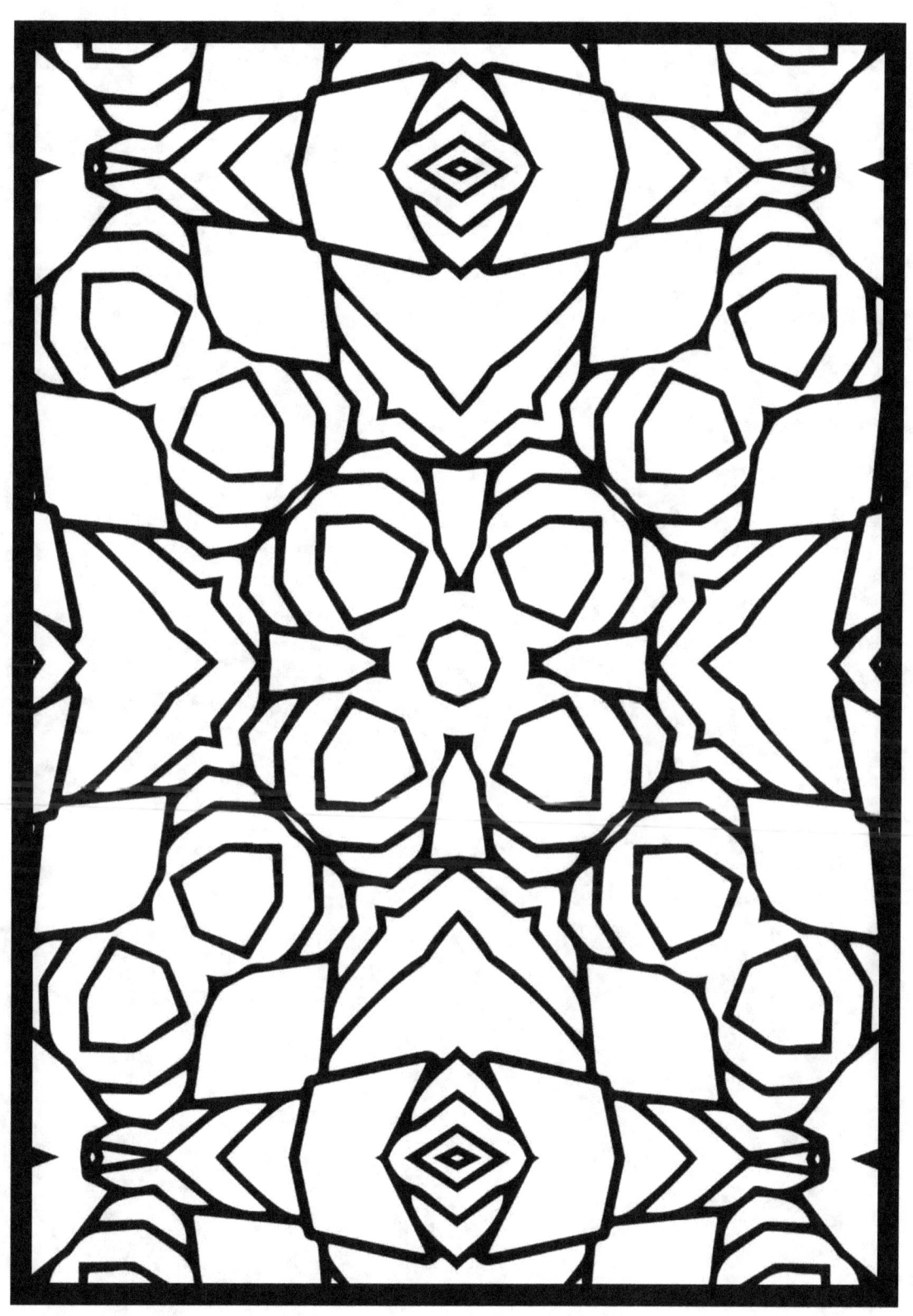

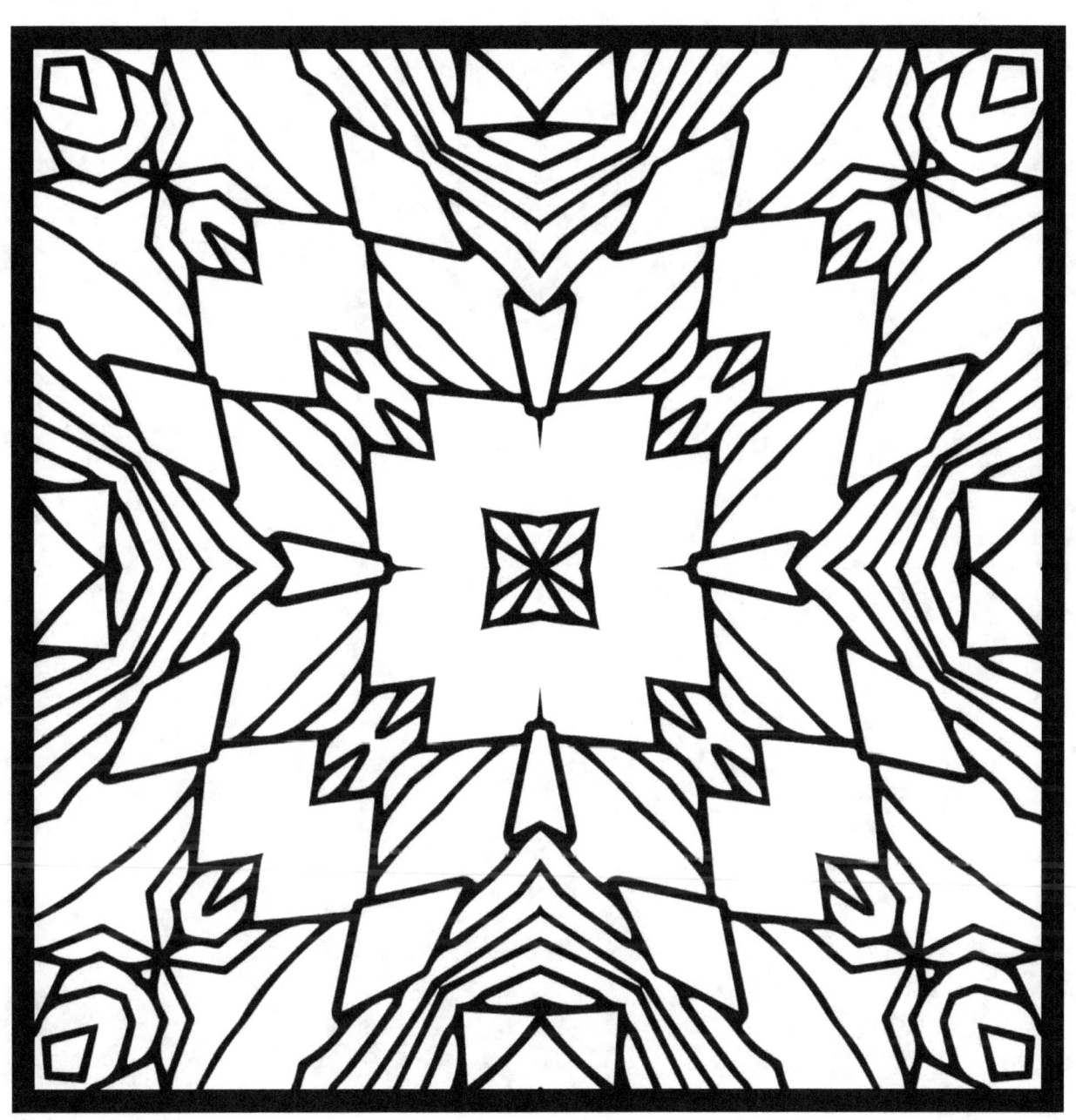

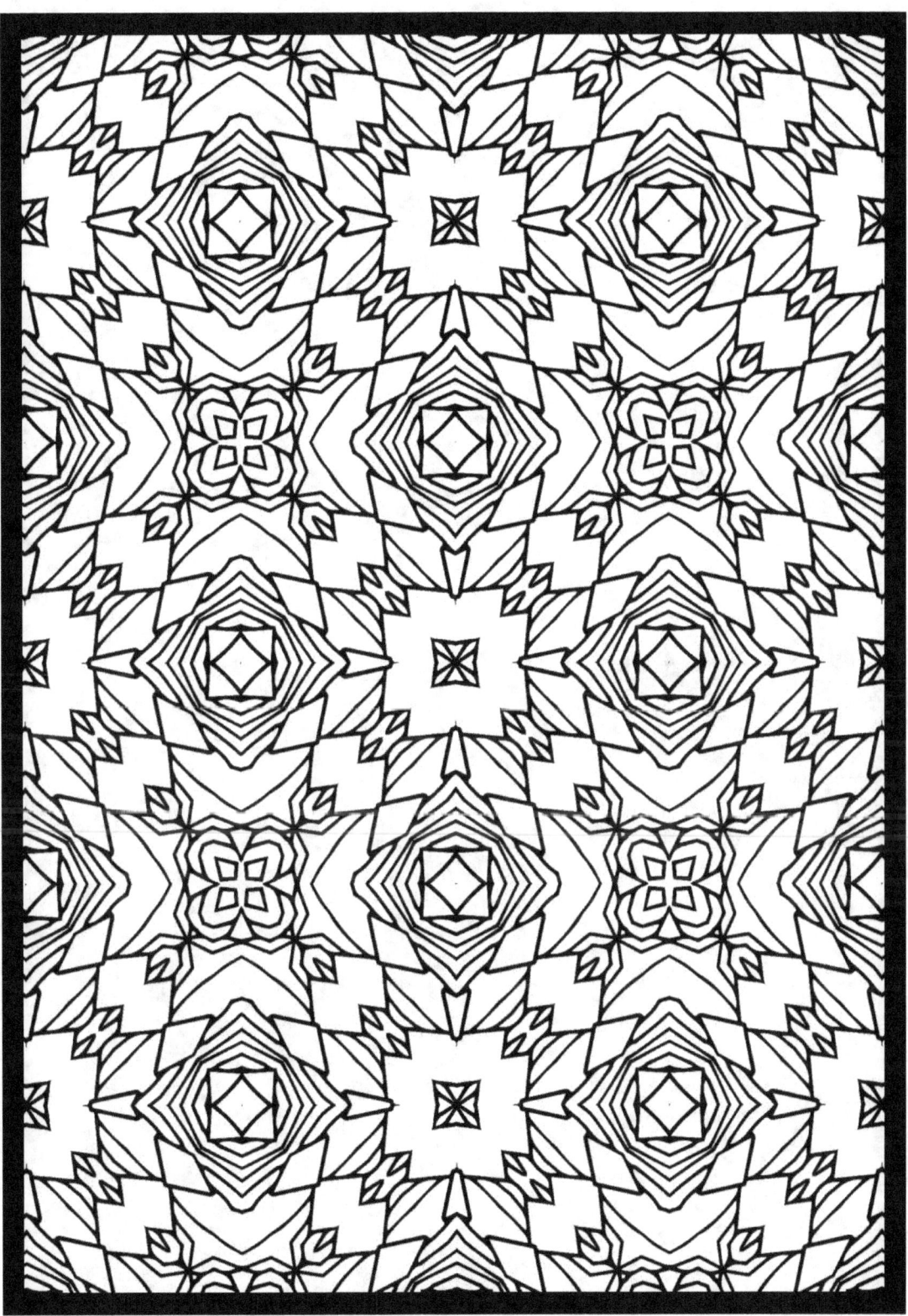

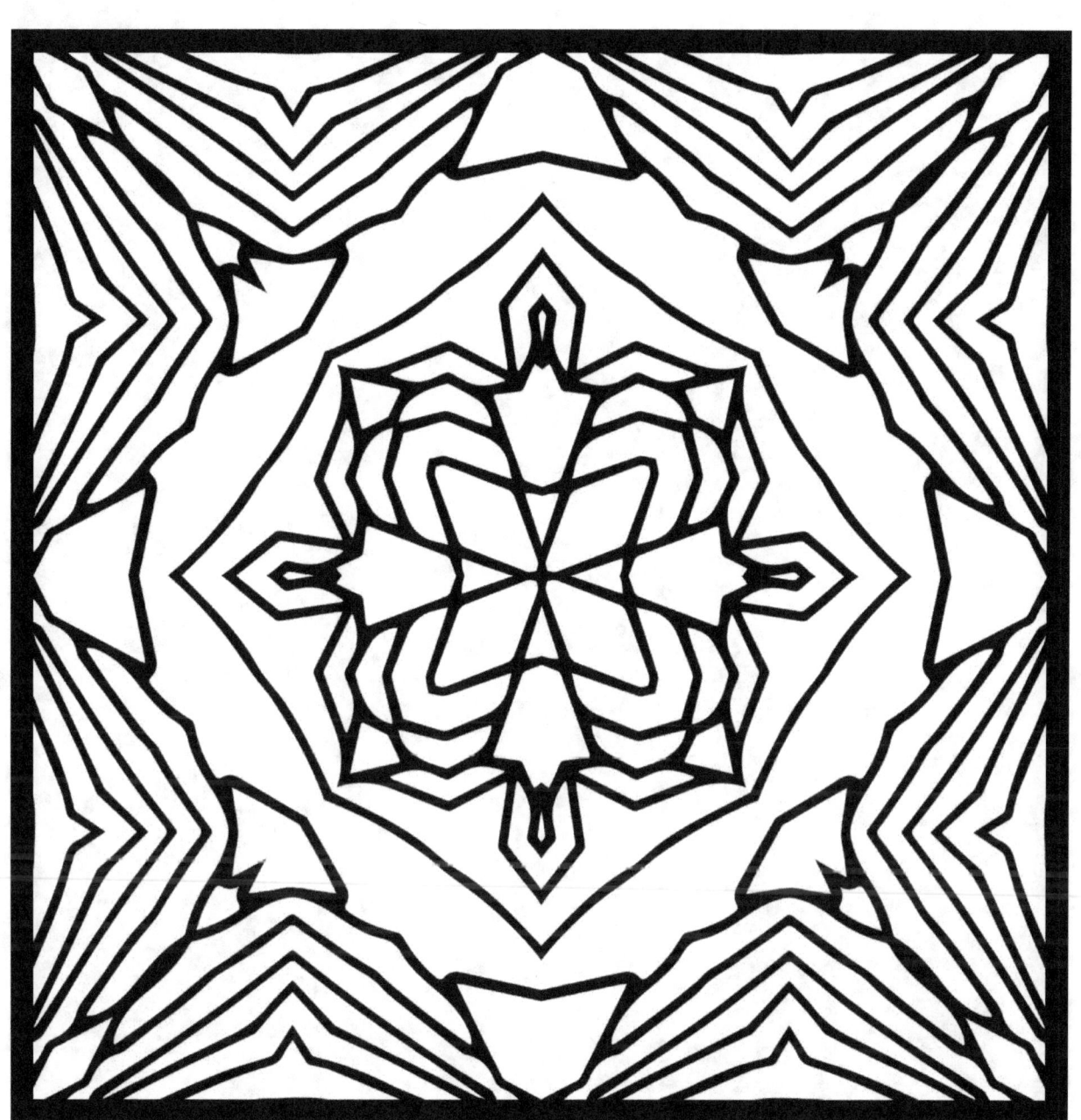

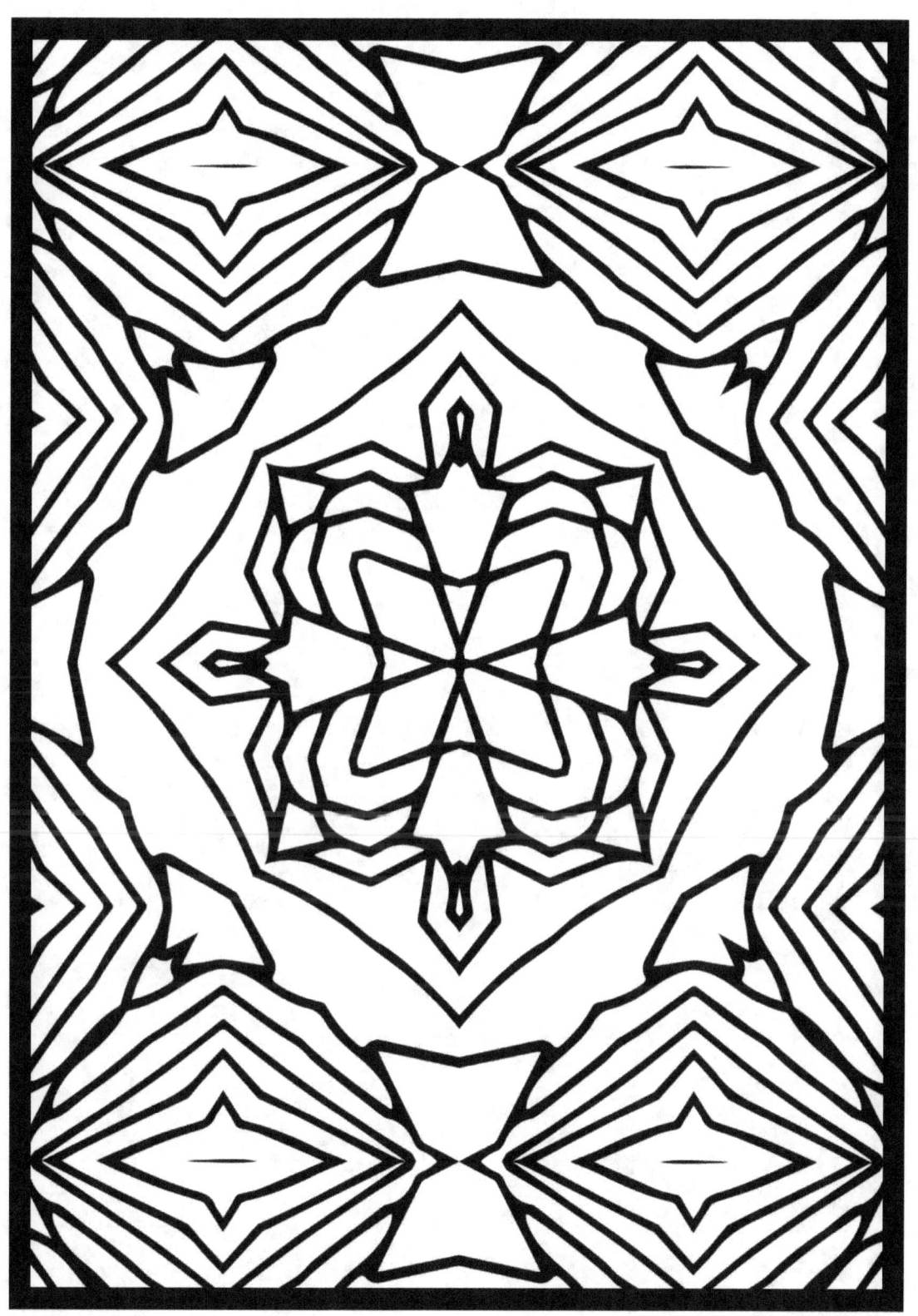

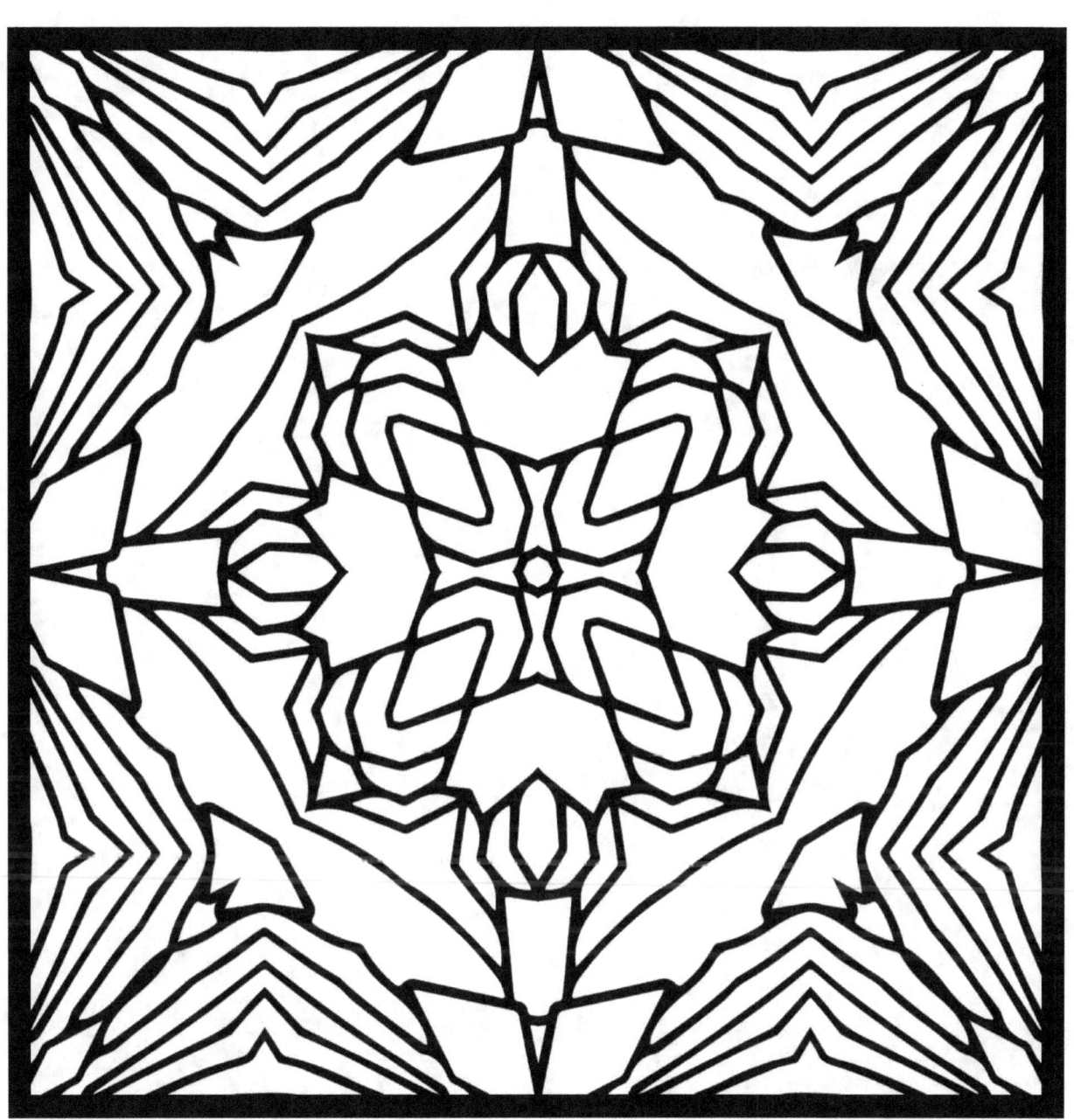

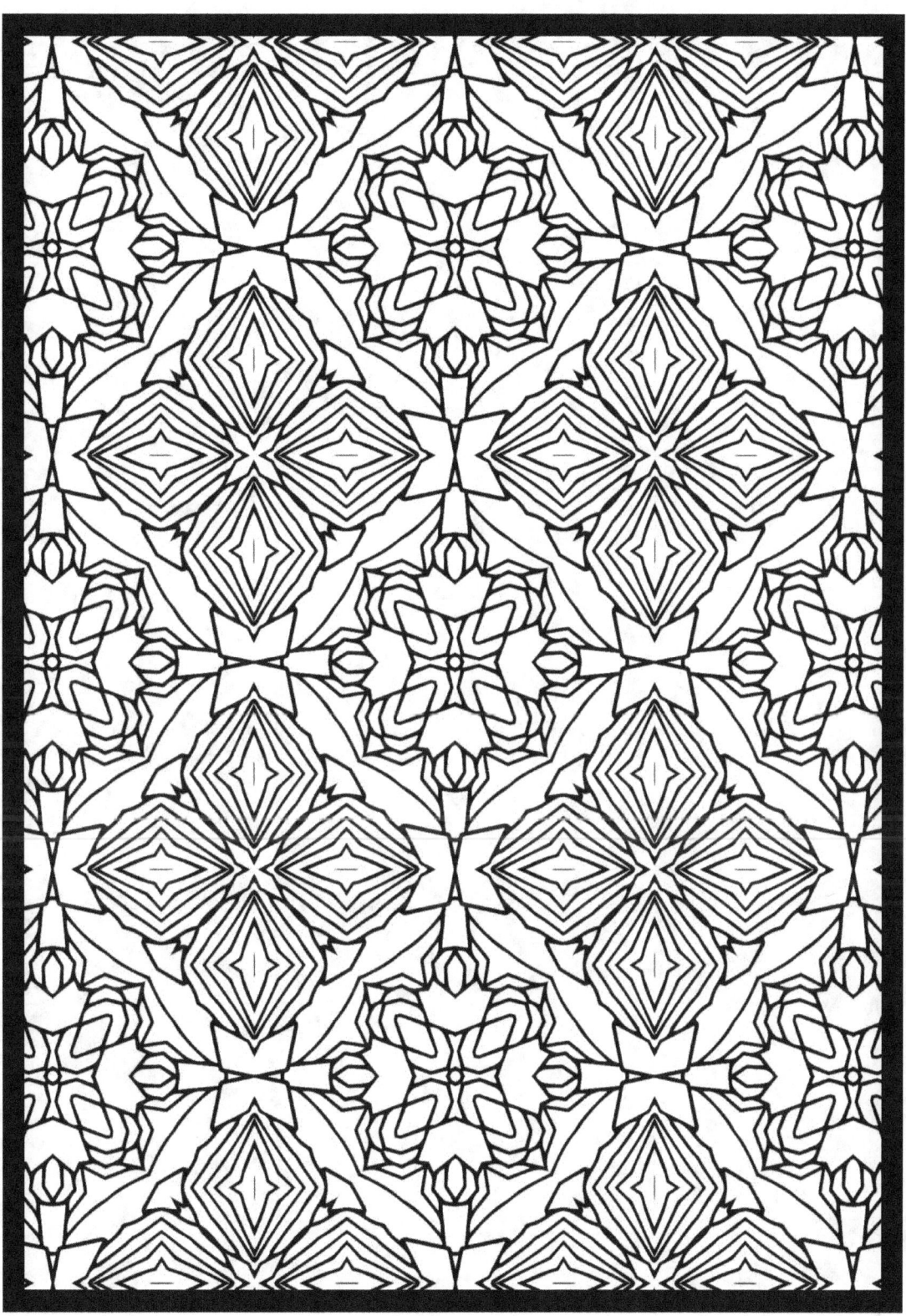

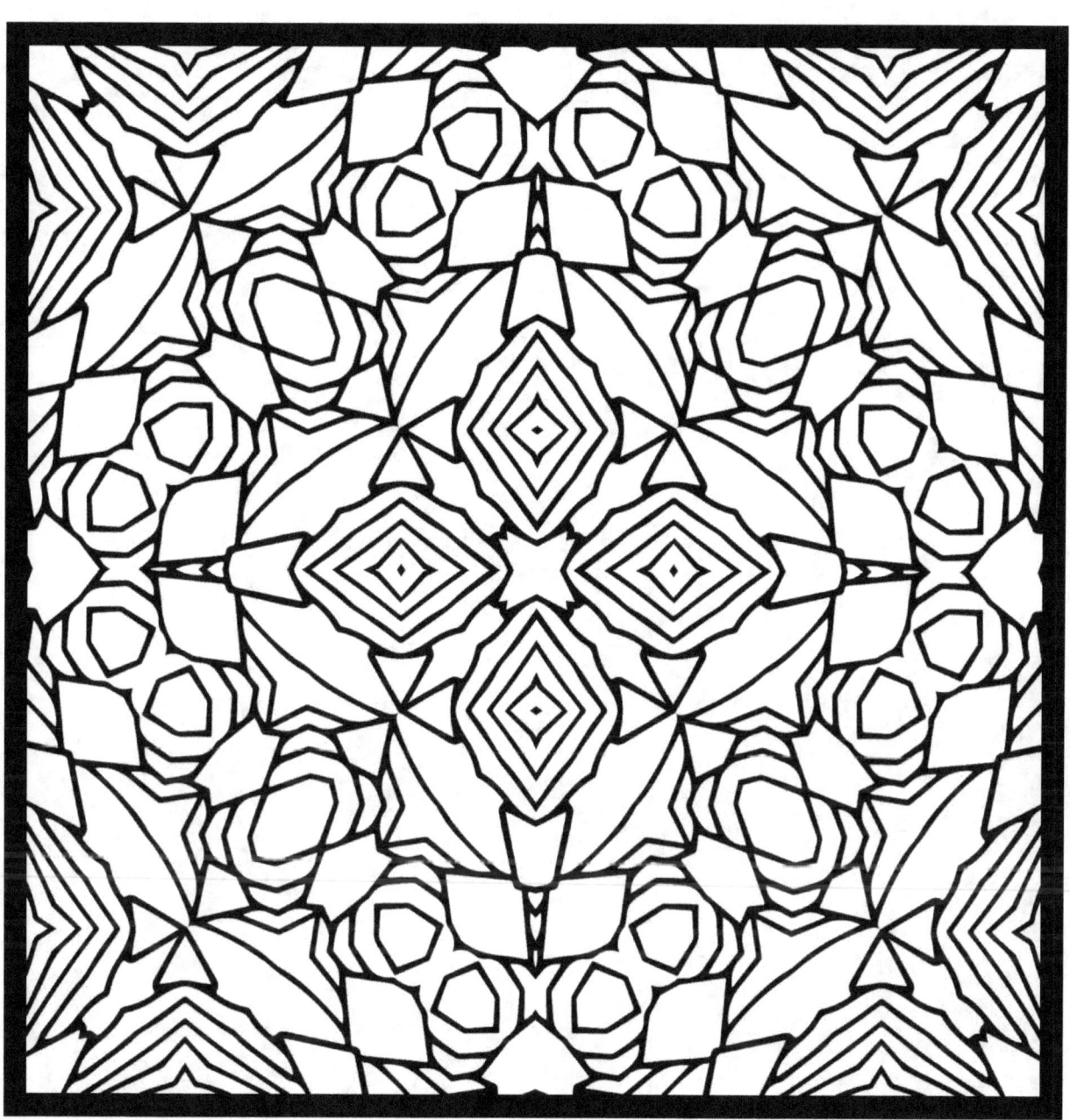

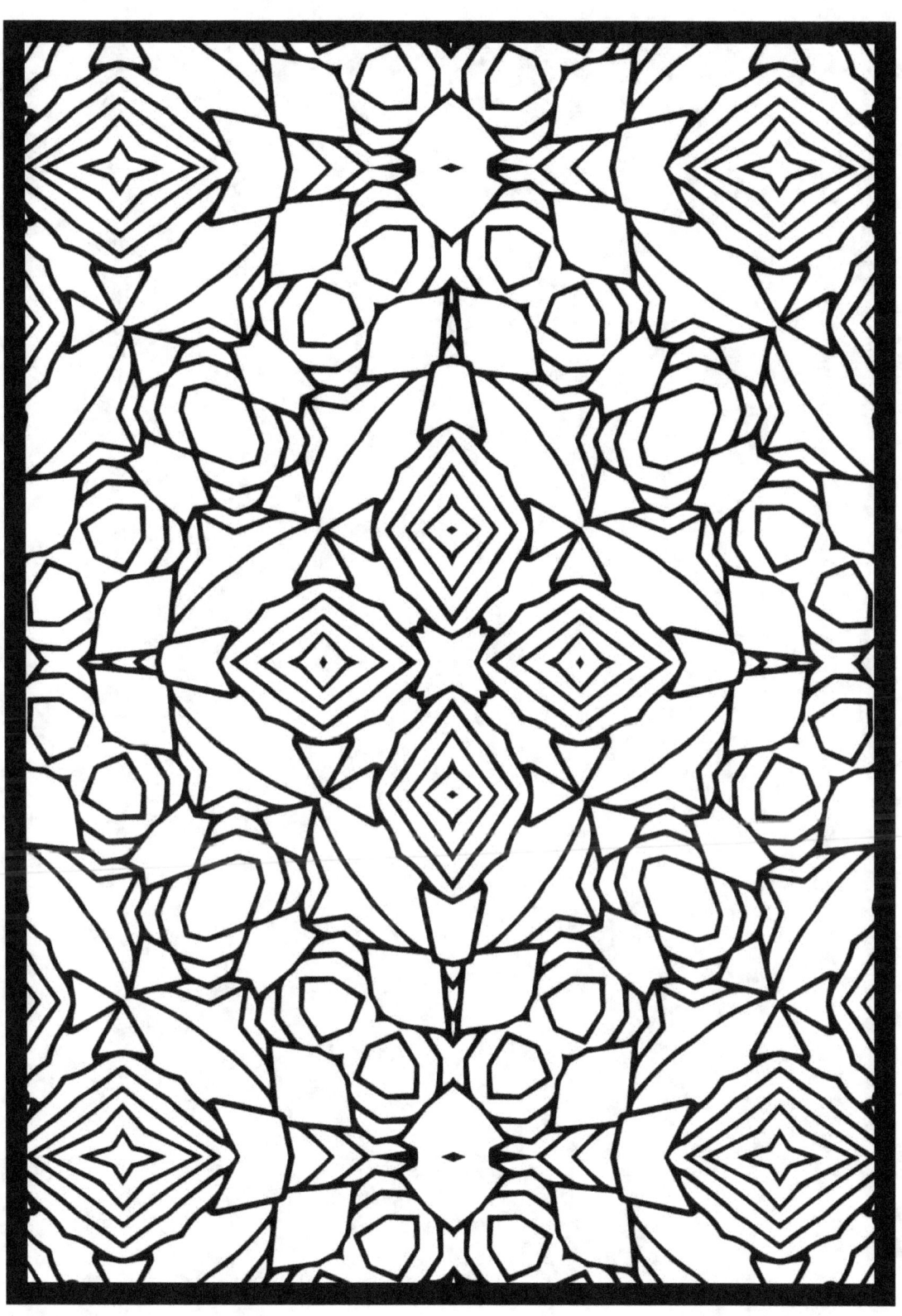

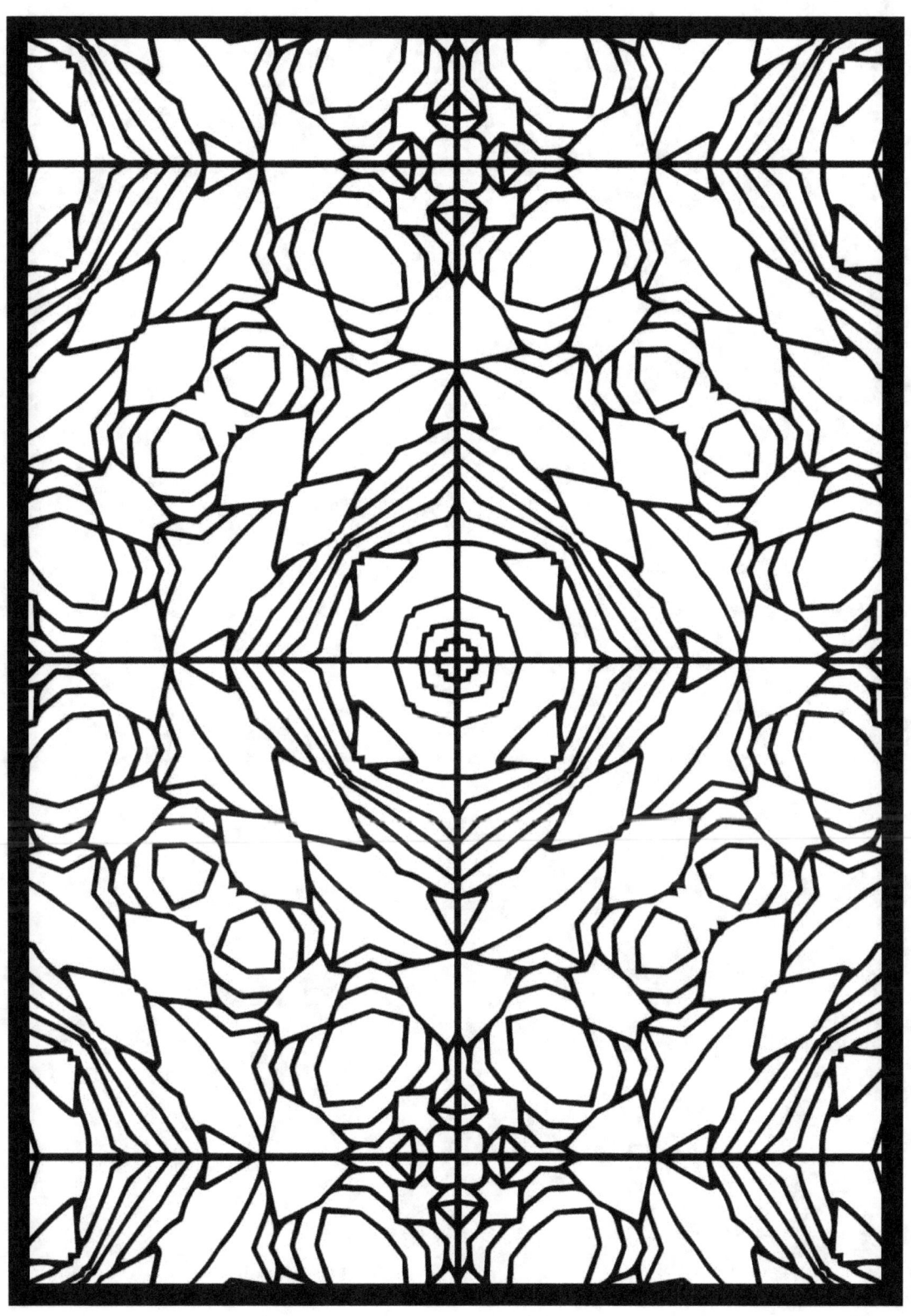

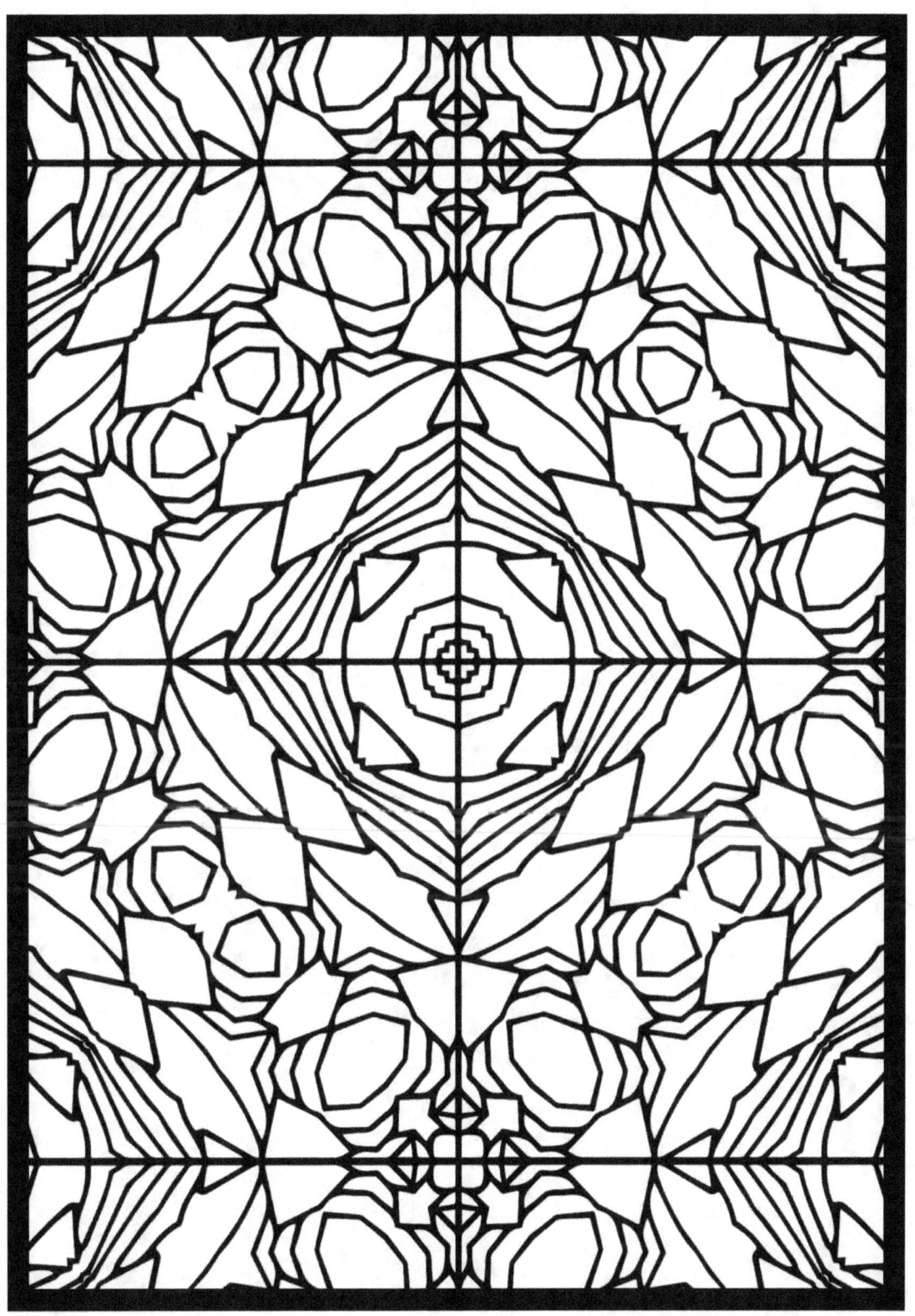

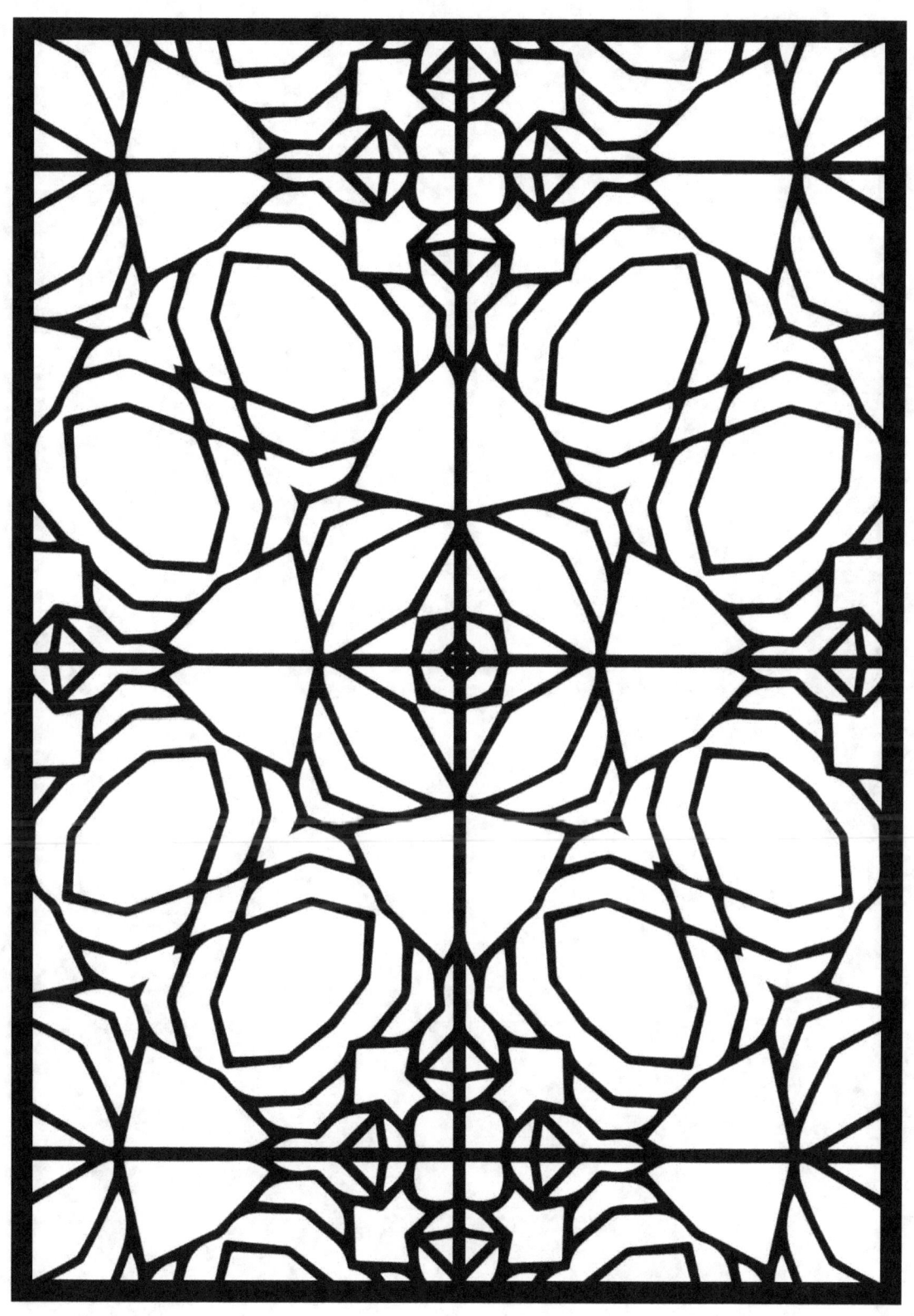

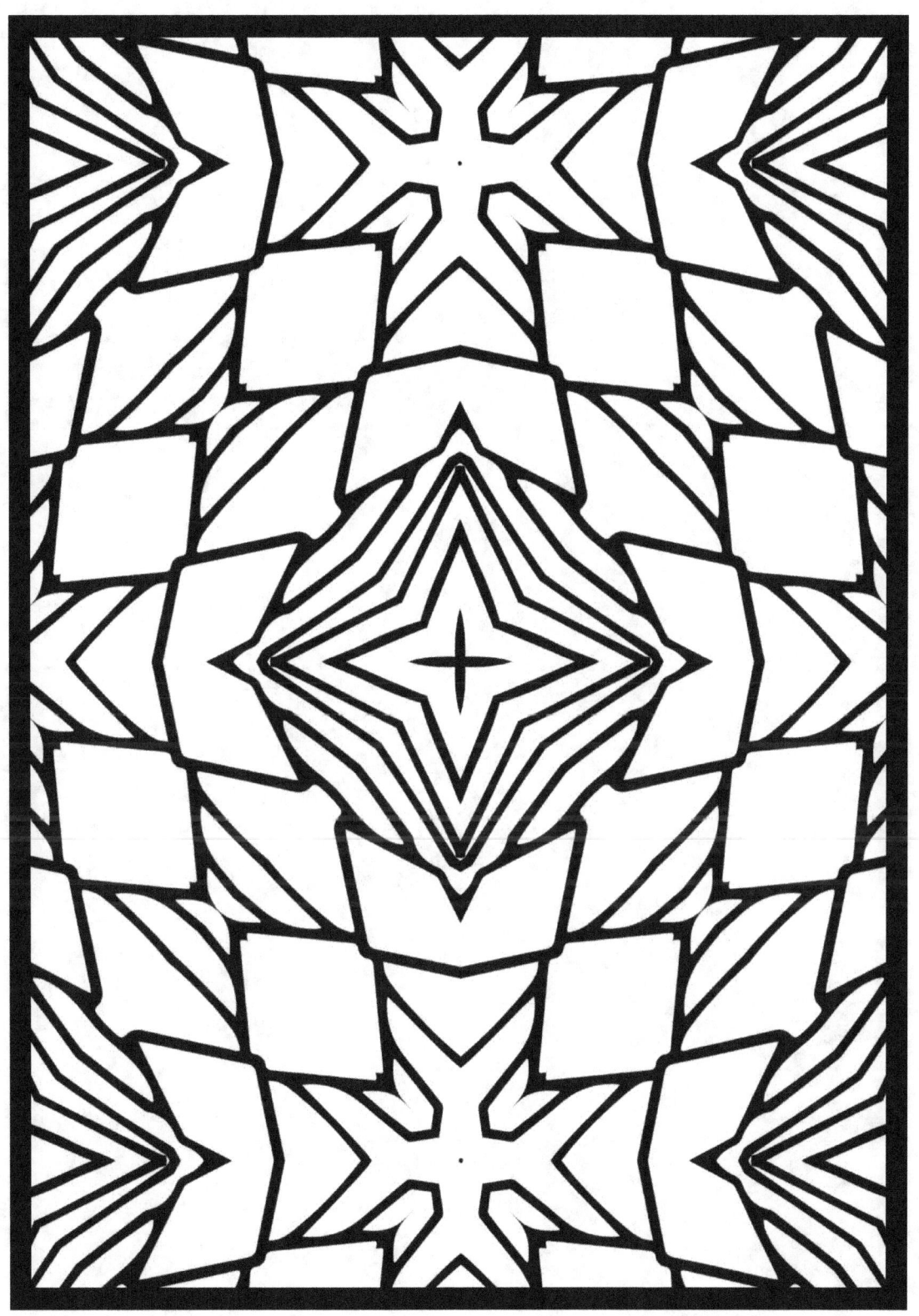

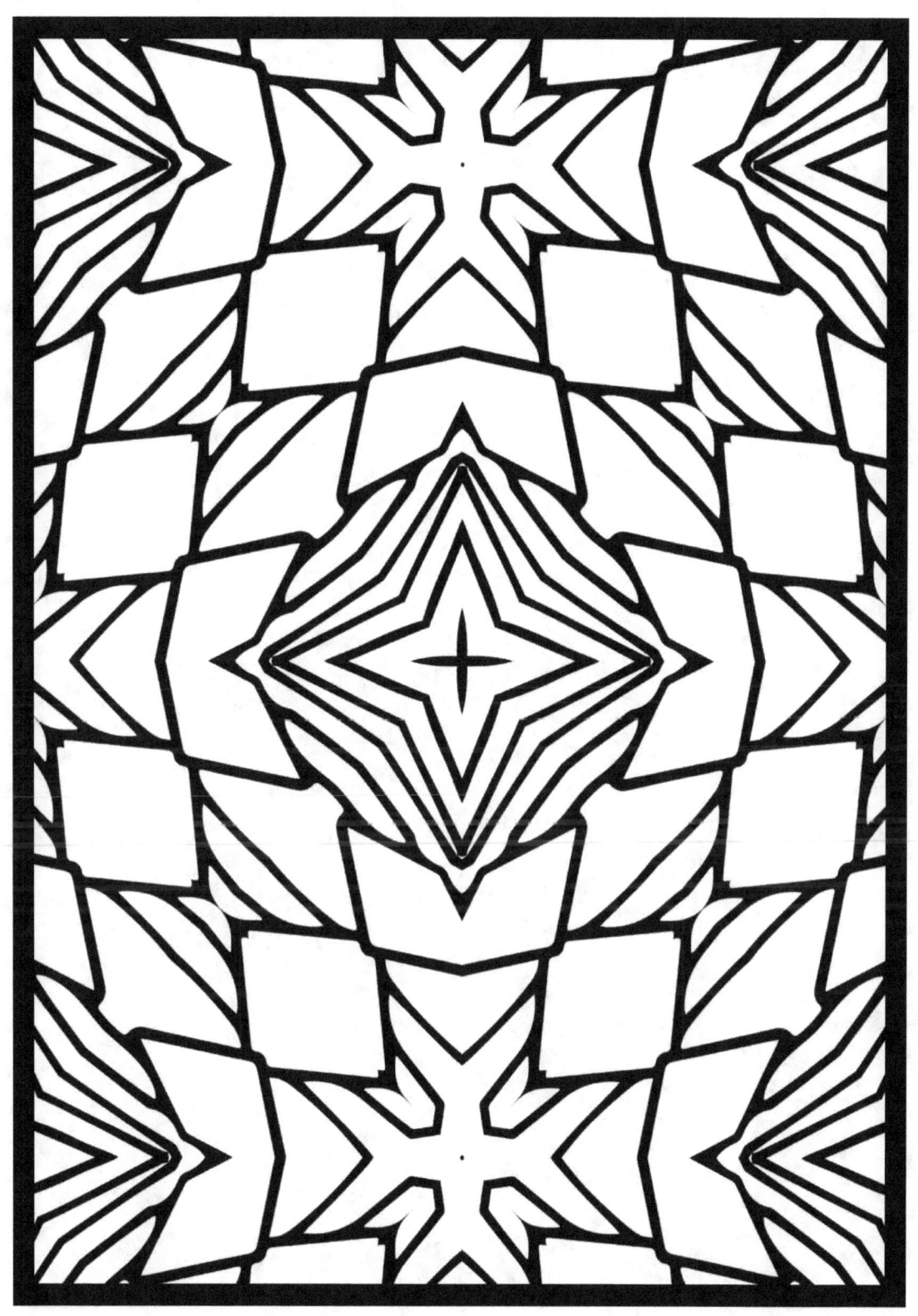

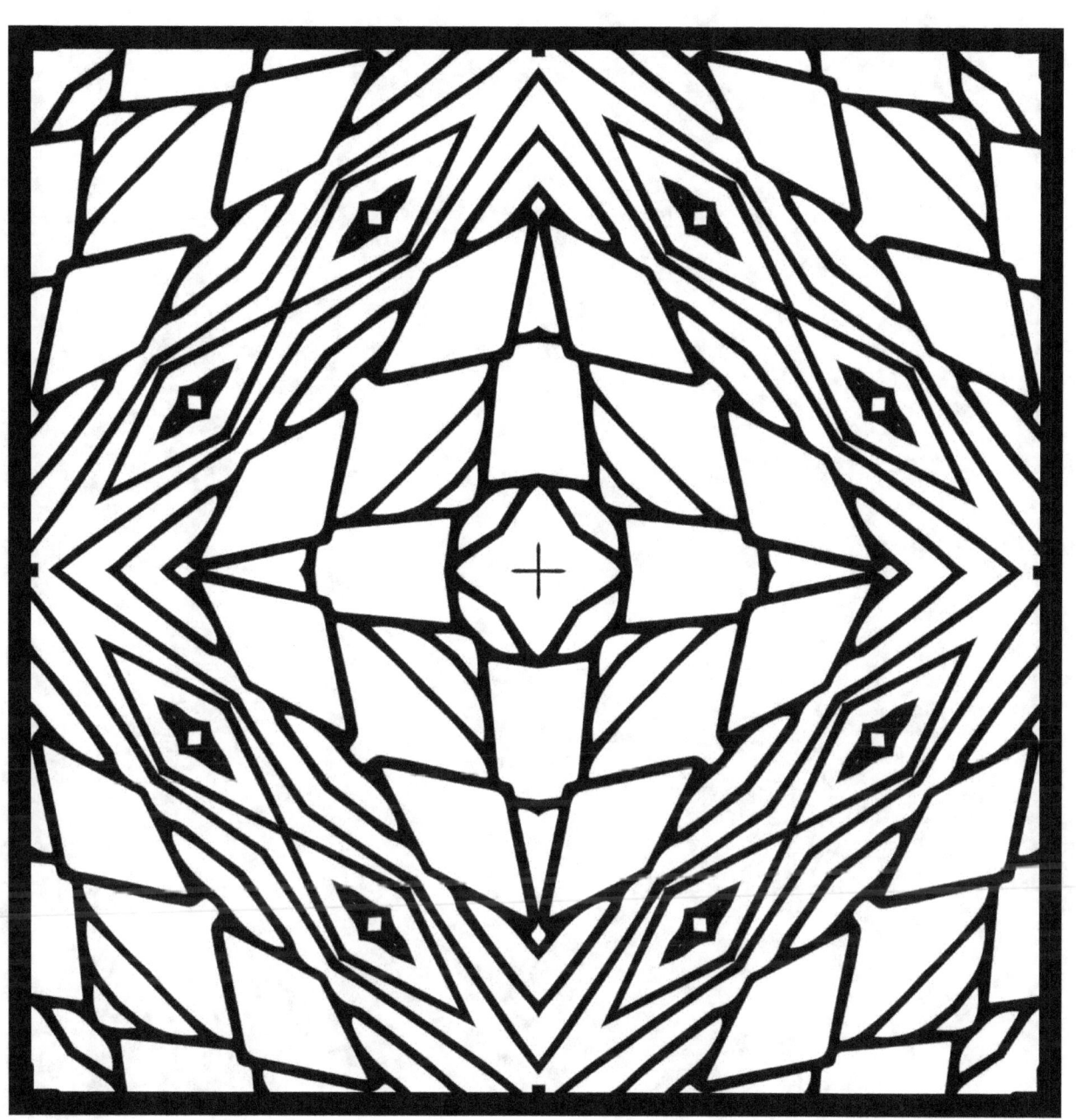

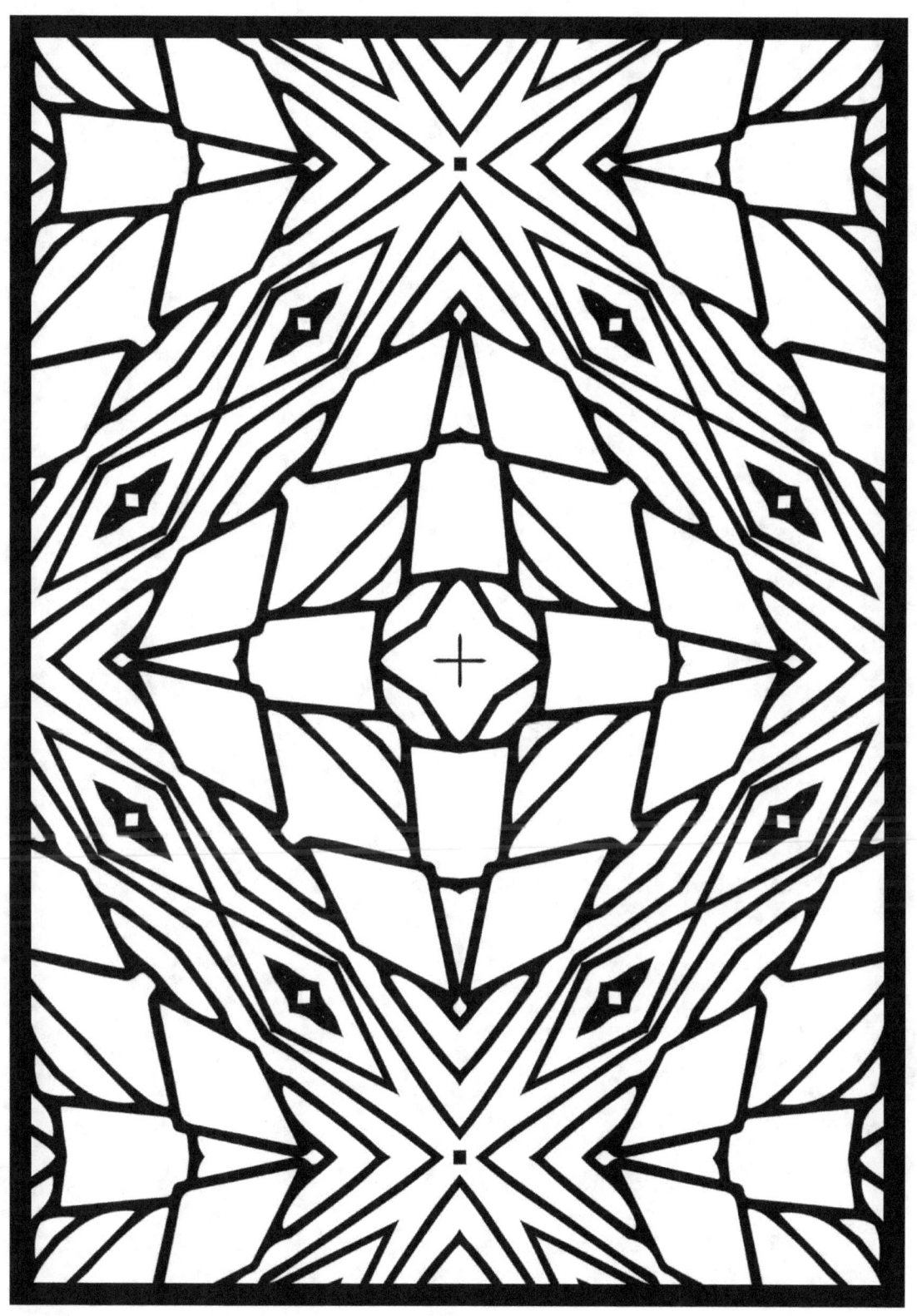

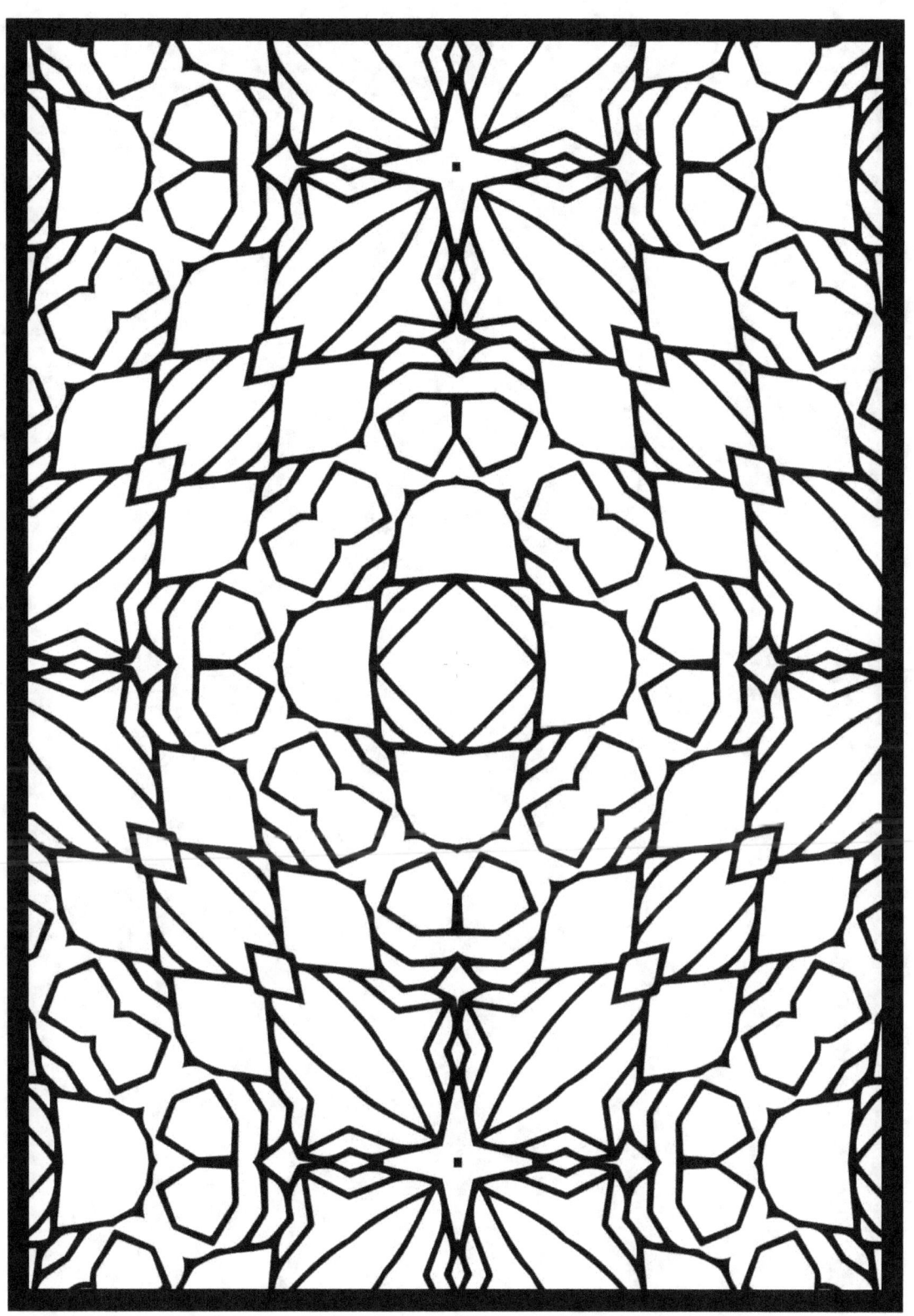

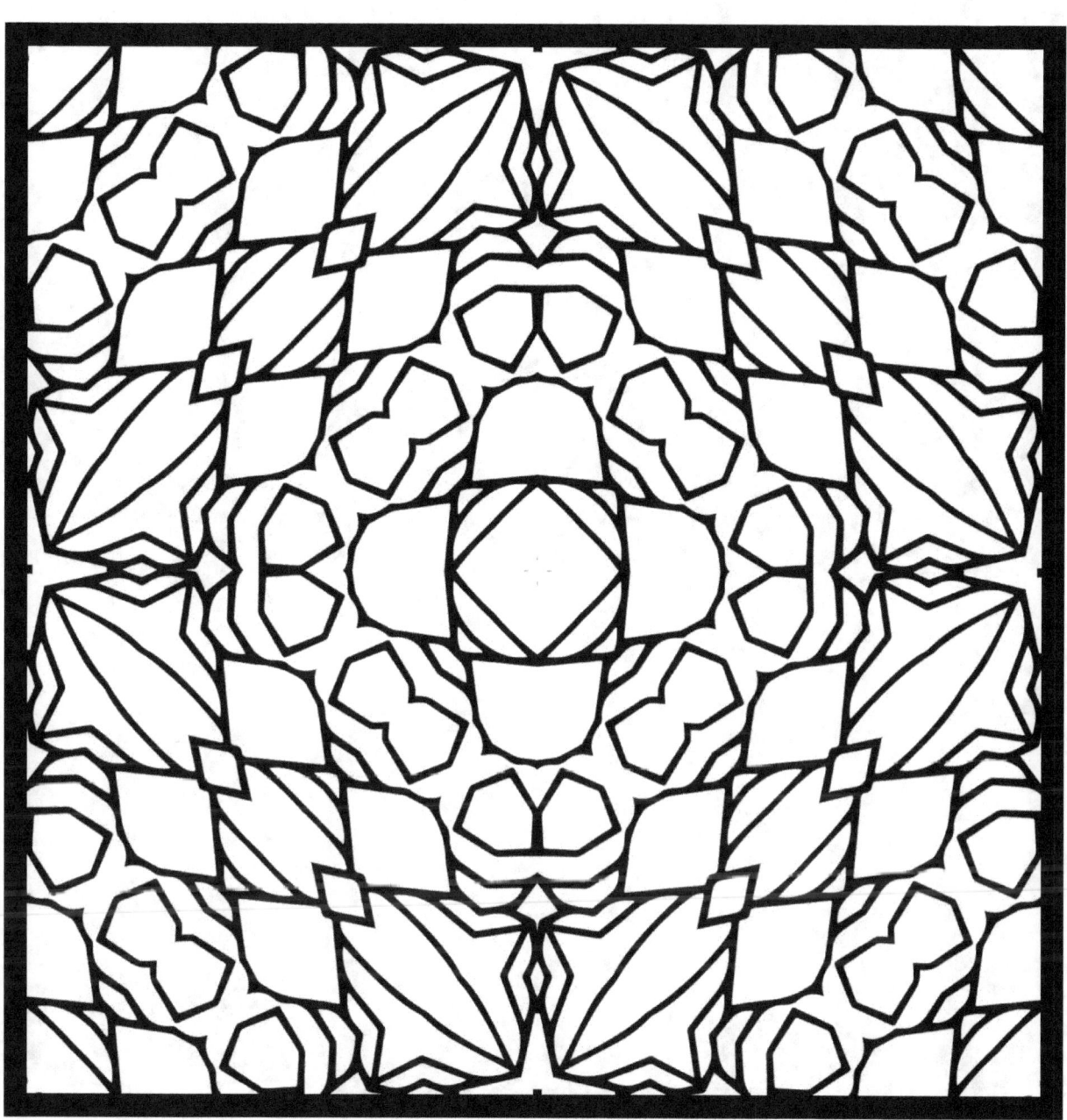

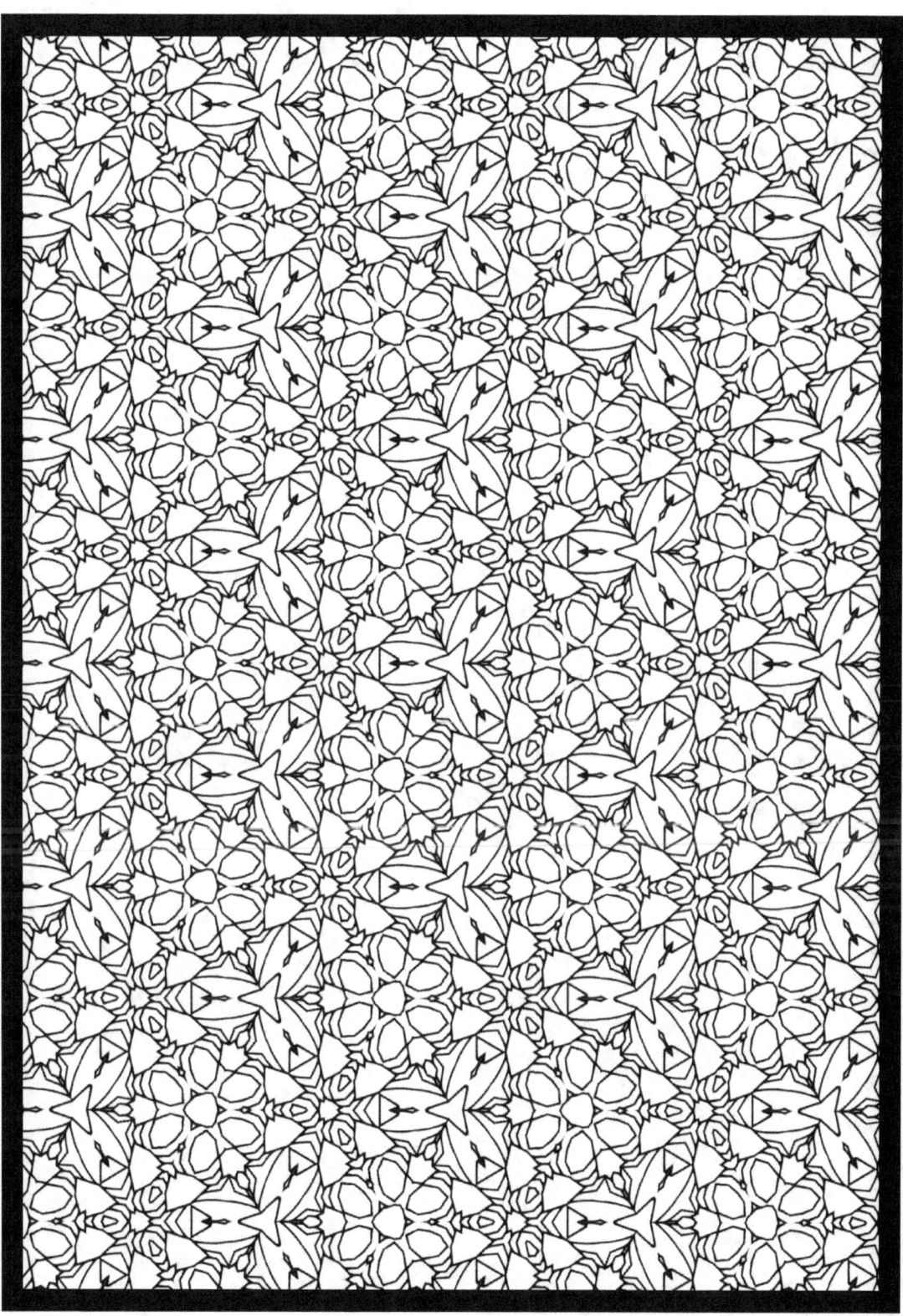

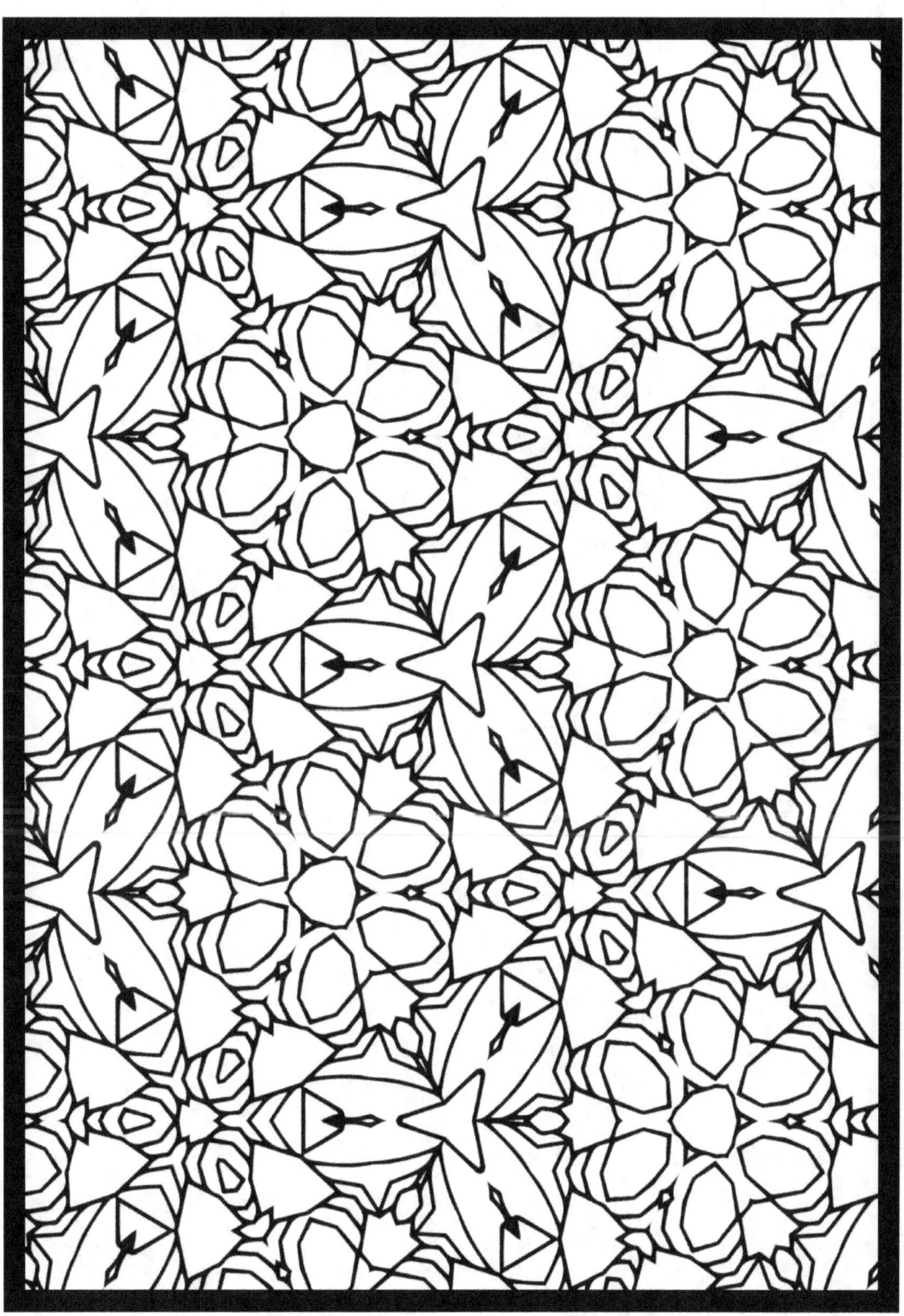

Coloring books by Gary Wittmann

30 Days of Coloring Books For Kids and Adult: Coloring Books For Adult (Volume 1)

30 Days of Coloring Books for Kids and Adults Volume 2 Snowflakes: Snowflakes

30 Days of Coloring Books for Kids and Adults Book 3 Patterns and Tiles: Relaxing Coloring, (Volume 3)

30 Days of Coloring Books for Kids and Adults Lovely Lions Grayscale Photo Book: **Lovely Lions Book 1** Grayscale Coloring Book

30 Days Of Coloring Books For Kids And Adults Bearly Beautiful: Bearly Beautiful Grayscale Photo Coloring Book (Volume 3)

30 Days of Coloring Book for Kids and Adult Dubois County Portrait Pictures: Dubois County Coloring Book Vol. 1 Portrait Pictures (Volume 1)

Thank you for purchasing the coloring book by Gary Wittmann. Please take a few minutes to write a review. This helps me to get the future books with your ideals and drawings in them.

www.ingramcontent.com/pod-product-compliance
Lightning Source LLC
Chambersburg PA
CBHW081731220526
45468CB00008B/2054